JAN   2014

Six Ingredients

Or Less®

Slow Cooker

Also by Carlean Johnson:

Six Ingredients or Less

Six Ingredients or Less Light & Healthy

Six Ingredients or Less Pasta & Casseroles

Six Ingredients or Less Low Carb

Six Ingredients or Less Diabetic

Six Ingredients or Less Families on the Go

Six

Ingredients

Or Less®

Slow Cooker

Carlean Johnson

CJ
Books
Washington

Six Ingredients or Less® Slow Cooker

Cover Design by Judy Petry
Cover Photos by Milkie Studios
Illustrations by Donald W. Harris
Final production design and editing by Linda Hazen
Typography and production by Katie Church
Editing by Corbett Petersen

Library of Congress Catalog Card Number: 2002093219
ISBN: 0-942878-06-X
CJ Books
PO Box 339
Moyie Springs, ID 83845
1-800-423-7184
www.sixingredientsorless.com
email: info@sixingredientsorless.com

Dedication

This book is dedicated to the memory of my twin brother Carlos Warren, whom I dearly miss, to my brother Conrad Warren, and to my sons Mike and Steve Johnson - three men in my life who I think just may enjoy the benefits of slow cooking.

Acknowledgements

I should first acknowledge all my Six Ingredients or Less customers. They are the ones who determine my next book and without their insistence I probably would never had written a slow cooker cookbook. I wasn't sure I wanted to write another book so quickly after my last one, but they were persistent and here it is.

I want to thank my family, neighbors, and especially friends Dorothy Lovelace Janice Stattin and Connie Owen. Writing a cookbook and meeting a deadline doesn't leave a lot of time for socializing, especially when you do two books back-to-back. I am eternally grateful for their patience and for hanging in there with me.

Katie Church, in addition to running the office, typed all the recipes and set the text as well. That is not an easy job. Thank you, Katie. I have someone new to introduce to you. We have a new illustrator this time around. Donald Harris is not only Katie's brother-in-law, but is an architect in California. This is his other talent. Thanks Donald, for taking time out of a very busy schedule to do the illustrations for this book.

By now you are probably familiar with the name Judy Petry. She has designed all my cookbook covers and thankfully was able to also design the cover on this one. Judy is not only wonderful to work with, but has also become a dear friend. I also want to thank Fred and Paul Milkie of Milkie Studios who did the beautiful photo shots for the cover.

A big thank you to my daughter Linda Hazen for everything she has contributed to this book. And for taking time out from being a busy mom to make sure we met our deadline. A big thank you to my granddaughter Paulina for the hours spent proofreading. I'm not sure that's how you wanted to spend your free time, but I really appreciated your help.

Also, last but not least, I want to thank Corbett Petersen for coming to our rescue and making it possible for us to meet our deadline. And to Rival® for allowing us to use their Rival® Crock-Pot® slow cookers for our cover photographs.

Carlean Johnson

Table of Contents

Slow Cooking

A Little Something Extra

Introduction

Slow cooking has become a way of life - again! Slow Cookers have been taken out, dusted off, and put to good use in numerous homes across the country.

Slow cookers first became popular in 1971 and enjoyed that popularity for several years before being stored in a closet or showing up at garage sales. With today's busy life-styles, slow cooking is again the answer to putting hot food on the table at our convenience.

This is a collection of recipes that I have enjoyed in my home and now I pass them on to you. Make them your recipes by following the recipes as presented, or adding or omitting ingredients to suit your taste.

Happy Slow Cooking!

Carlean

About the Author

Carlean Johnson, mother of four, resides in scenic Gig Harbor in the Puget Sound area of Washington State. Her love of cooking inspired her to write a series of Six Ingredients or Less cookbooks. She also gives cooking lessons and lectures on quick and easy cooking to fit today's busy lifestyles.

Slow Cooker Basics

If there is one sure thing I have learned about slow cooking, it is that each slow cooker has it's own personality. Actually just like our ovens, only not as easily resolved. Each slow cooker I tested cooked at a different temperature, even identical models made by the same company.

You can check how hot your slow cooker cooks by filling it with 2 quarts of water; cover and heat on LOW for 8 hours. Then use an accurate thermometer to check the temperature. The ranges I found were from 185° to 218° with the 185° degree slow cooker as the one I liked best. If yours is in the 200° range, you know yours will cook somewhat fast, Anything above that and you will need to watch the food and check cooking times more carefully. I know today's models cook much faster than yesterdays. If you have just purchased a new slow cooker, check the temperature as directed above. If it cooks much too hot, I would return it and try another one. After all, the purpose of slow cooking is "slow cooking".

If you are happy with your slow cooker, use the recipes in this book as a guideline. Each time you make a recipe for the first time, jot down the cooking time. If you have more than one slow cooker, also write down the one you used. This information will be extremely important the next time around.

Slow cookers come in different shapes and sizes. There are two I personally like to use. One is a round 5 quart slow cooker. This works best for small and medium size recipes. The other one is a 5½ quart oval slow cooker. This works great for large recipes, large casseroles, and oval shaped meats. I wouldn't suggest anything smaller than a 3 to 3½ quart size. A 5 to 6 quart size might be best for a large family or if you do a lot of cooking. If you have a slow cooker that switches to a warm setting, all the better.

---

1 hour on HIGH equals 2 hours on LOW

Power Out!

If the power goes out and you are at home, remove the food and continue cooking by other means, if possible. If this happens and you aren't at home, you should throw the food away even if it appears to be done.

Things to Remember

BROWN or not to brown the food is sometimes up to you. I avoided pre-browning as much as possible. If the recipes in this book say to brown, I felt it was necessary.

LIQUID does not evaporate in a slow cooker-it accumulates. Almost all foods contain water so you actually end up with more water than when you started.

OVERCOOKING - Regardless of what some companies and cookbooks tell you, it is possible to overcook or burn food in a slow cooker. That is why it is so important to know how fast your slow cooker cooks. Today's slow cookers cook much faster than our grandmothers' did and we need to take that into account. Cooking times vary from company to company, and from slow cooker to slow cooker. Overcooked food will eventually take on an odd taste or flavor and some casseroles can actually start to burn around the edges. It is important to check the food at the minimum cooking time, especially the first time you make a recipe.

COOKING TIMES can be easily adjusted in slow cooking. You can cook the entire time on LOW or HIGH or you can start out on low, then finish cooking on HIGH. Or start out on HIGH and later reduce to LOW. In some recipes that use eggs and bread, you may find it best to cook on HIGH the entire time.

YOUR RECIPES can sometimes be adjusted and cooked in a slow cooker. In most cases, except for rice, you will need to use about half the liquid called for in the recipe. Sometimes you just have to experiment, to see if your recipe will work.

CREAMED SOUPS and processed cheese are used in some of the recipes since they work so well in slow cooking. They replace milk and cream that can sometimes curdle and cheese that can separate if cooked too long.

Appetizers & Beverages

Appetizers

Appetizers and beverages made in a slow cooker are unbelievably easy to make and a boon to the busy cook. Entertaining is made easier by the mere fact that once assembled in the pot most recipes can be left unattended until ready to serve.

Most of the recipes can be served from the slow cooker and will keep hot for several hours if kept on "warm." If your slow cooker doesn't have a warm setting, use the "low" setting and check occasionally to see if the food needs a quick stir to prevent overcooking or drying out.

You will enjoy the delicious dips in this section, and if you like Brie, you must try the Raspberry - Almond Brie on page 18; it makes a great holiday appetizer, and is so easy to make. The beverages are also nice because you can just heat and serve from the slow cooker.

Beef & Salsa Dip

1	pound lean ground beef
16	ounces process cheese spread, cubed
1	can (15-ounces) creamed corn
1½	cups salsa

Brown ground beef; drain and add to slow cooker along with cheese and remaining ingredients. Cook on HIGH 1 to 1½ hours or until cheese is melted and mixture is hot. Turn heat to LOW, until ready to serve, stirring occasionally. Serve with chips. Makes 5½ cups.

This is so good I doubt you will have leftovers, but if you do, serve over baked potatoes for a quick and easy lunch or dinner.

Cheese & Chili Dip

1	package (12-ounces) hot or spicy sausage
16	ounces process cheese spread, cubed
1	can (15-ounces) chili without beans

Cook sausage in a medium skillet; drain off fat.

Meanwhile, place cheese in a sprayed slow cooker. Add sausage and chili. Cover and cook on LOW 1½ to 2 hours or until heated through and cheese has melted, stirring once as the cheese melts. Do not continue to cook or mixture will become too thick. Serve hot.

Variation: Add sliced black olives. This dish is quite spicy and salty. You could substitute ground beef for the sausage.

Note: Since you are only heating the ingredients in the slow cooker, you want to make sure the sausage is cooked through, not just browned.

Chili con Queso

A popular recipe made easy in a slow cooker.

1   pound lean ground beef
1   cup chopped onion
1   can (4-ounces) chopped green chilies
1   cup chunky salsa
2   pounds process cheese spread, cubed

Brown ground beef and onion; drain. Place in slow cooker. Add remaining ingredients. Cover and cook on LOW 2 to 3 hours, stirring to blend when cheese is partially melted. Makes about 6 cups.

Hot Artichoke Dip

If you want to make a crowd happy and promote conversation, gather them around this delicious hot dip.

1   can (9-ounces) artichoke hearts, drained
1   can (4-ounces) chopped green chilies
1   cup mayonnaise
1   cup freshly grated Parmesan cheese

Combine ingredients in a sprayed small slow cooker. Cover and cook on LOW 1 hour or until heated through. Watch carefully after 30 minutes; if overheated the mixture can separate.

Note: If you don't have a small slow cooker, you may want to double the recipe. If you are in a hurry, heat mixture in a saucepan and add to the slow cooker to keep hot.

Variation: Add chopped chicken, shrimp or crab.

Nacho-Salsa Cheese Sauce

16 ounces process cheese spread, cubed
2 cups (8-ounces) Cheddar cheese, shredded
3½ cups medium or hot chunky salsa
1 cup sliced ripe olives

Combine all the ingredients in a sprayed slow cooker. Cover and cook on LOW 3 to 4 hours or until heated through and cheese has melted. Makes about 8 cups.

Cheesy Bean Dip

2 pounds lean ground beef
1 cup chunky salsa, drained thoroughly
1 can (16-ounces) white beans, drained
1 can (15-ounces) chili beans, drained
4 Cups (16-ounces) Cheddar cheese, shredded

Brown ground beef; drain. Add to a sprayed slow cooker along with the salsa and beans. Stir in about three fourths of the cheese. Sprinkle remaining cheese on top. Cover and cook on LOW 2 hours or until heated through. Makes about 8 cups.

Leftovers: Serve in soft tortillas topped with salsa and then rolled. Or place filled tortillas in a casserole, sprinkle with cheese and bake until heated through. Serve with additional salsa, if desired.

Peppy Refried Bean Dip

1 can (16-ounces) refried beans
1 can (10-ounces) Tomatoes & Green Chilies, drained

Combine ingredients in a sprayed small slow cooker. Cover and cook on LOW about 2 hours or until heated through. Makes 2 cups.

Raspberry-Almond Brie

This appetizer will WOW your guests. It is absolutely delicious. Serve with butter crackers or cubed French bread.

1   round (16-ounces) Brie cheese
1½ tablespoons raspberry preserves
1   tablespoon packed light brown sugar
1   tablespoon sliced almonds

Remove top rind only from Brie. Place in a shallow dish as close to the size of the Brie as possible. I have a 7-inch pie tin that works perfectly for this. Spread top of cheese with preserves. Sprinkle with brown sugar and then the almonds. Place in slow cooker. Cover and cook on LOW 1½ to 2 hours or until heated through. Do not overcook or the mixture will be too runny.

Sweet & Sour Meatballs

Note: It is necessary to cook this on HIGH in order to thicken the sauce.

2   pounds lean ground beef
2   cups ketchup
1   cup packed light brown sugar
1   tablespoon prepared mustard
2   teaspoons Worcestershire sauce
2   teaspoons soy sauce

Shape ground beef into 1-inch balls and place in a shallow baking pan. Bake at 425° for 15 minutes or until meat is lightly browned. Drain on paper towels and place in a sprayed slow cooker.

Combine remaining ingredients with ¼ cup water and pour over the meatballs. Cover and cook on HIGH 1½ to 2 hours or until sauce has thickened. Serve with toothpicks. Makes 60 meatballs.

White Chocolate Hot Chocolate

2	cups heavy whipping cream
6	cups whole or 2% milk
12	ounces white chocolate
1	teaspoon vanilla extract

Enjoy a steaming cup of hot chocolate for dessert. Very rich and smooth.

Place ingredients in a slow cooker and heat on LOW 2 to 2½ hours or until chocolate is melted and mixture is hot; stir well to blend. Makes 10 cups.

Note: You need the whipping cream for taste and sweetness, but since it is so rich, I use the 2% milk instead of the whole milk. It is still very rich, you won't miss a thing.

Variation: Add 1 to 2 cups hot coffee or to taste. This should be added just before serving. If desired, garnish with shaved milk chocolate.

A slow cooker is convenient for hot beverages that can be made in the pot or added to the pot and kept hot.

Spiced Apple Cider

Who doesn't like a cup of hot apple cider and this one is so easy to make.

2	quarts full-bodied apple cider
2	cups pineapple juice
1	cup light corn syrup
15	whole cloves
3	cinnamon sticks
1	lemon, sliced

Combine all the ingredients in a slow cooker. Cover and cook on LOW about 3 hours. Makes about 10 cups.

Hot Cup of Cheer

This mixture can be made ahead and stored in the refrigerator for as long as a week. Reheat when needed.

1	cup sugar
12	whole cloves
2	pieces (2-inch) cinnamon sticks
6	cups grapefruit juice
3	cups orange juice
4	cups apple cider

In a medium saucepan, combine sugar, cloves, cinnamon sticks and ½ cup water. Bring to a boil, reduce heat and simmer 20 minutes. Remove cloves and cinnamon. Pour into a large slow cooker. Add the juice and cider. Cover and cook on LOW 2 to 3 hours to heat through. Depending on the grapefruit juice used this can be tart or sweet. Add additional sugar, if desired. Makes 26 punch cup servings.

Brunch and Soups

Brunch & Soups

Breakfast casseroles, stratas, quiche and numerous other egg dishes can be "baked" with excellent results in a slow cooker. The slow cooker also works well for keeping dishes hot such as the Heat & Hold Scrambled Eggs on page 25 and the Sausage & Gravy on page 24.

I have included a lot of soup recipes for the slow cooker. A great meal can be made with a steaming bowl of hot soup, a delicious hot roll or muffin and a salad or dessert. Most of the recipes are quite hardy and many can be frozen. All can be made ahead and reheated.

Brunch Ham & Cheese Casserole

2	cups (about 8-ounces) cubed ham
¼	cup sliced green onions (green and white part)
1	cup (4-ounces) Monterey Jack cheese with peppers, shredded
12	large eggs, lightly beaten
1	cup heavy whipping cream

Place ham in a sprayed slow cooker. Sprinkle with onion, then the cheese. Combine eggs and whipping cream with 1 cup water. Pour over cheese. Cover and cook on HIGH 2½ to 3 hours or until firm in the center. Makes 8 servings.

Makes a nice brunch or light supper dish. Serve with sausage, fruit salad and Crescent rolls. Quite good reheated.

Ham & Cheese Strata

1	loaf (8-ounces) French bread
1	cup cubed ham
1	cup (4-ounces) Swiss cheese, shredded
6	large eggs, lightly beaten
1	cup half and half
1	cup milk

Cut bread into about 1-inch size cubes and place in a sprayed slow cooker. Sprinkle ham and then cheese over top. Combine remaining ingredients until well mixed; pour over bread mixture. Cover and cook on HIGH 2½ to 3 hours or until mixture is set. Makes 6 servings.

Unless you are serving brunch or you get up really early, you will probably want to serve this for lunch or dinner. Just add a nice bowl of assorted fruits, some hot coffee, and if desired, some breakfast rolls or muffins.

Slow Cooker Oatmeal

Can be made a head and reheated. If desired, at serving time, add milk, sugar and cinnamon to flavor.

1¹/₃ cups old-fashioned oatmeal
2½ cups water
Dash of salt

Place ingredients in a sprayed slow cooker. Cover and cook on LOW 6 to 7 hours or until cooked through and creamy. Makes 3 to 4 servings.

Sausage Gravy

What a treat to have a recipe you can make ahead and keep hot in a slow cooker. You can then make the biscuits, which you must have when serving this dish. If you are really short on time or don't feel confident in making biscuits (see page 163) you could use canned biscuits such as Grands° or toast.

¾ pound sausage
¼ cup flour
2 cups milk
½ teaspoon salt
¼ teaspoon pepper

Brown sausage in a large skillet. Remove the sausage leaving the fat in the skillet; you will need 4 tablespoons. You may have to add some oil to make up the difference. Heat drippings until hot; add the flour and bring to a simmer, stirring until smooth. Add milk, salt and pepper. Cook, stirring frequently, until mixture has thickened. Add the sausage and place in a sprayed slow cooker. Cover and turn on LOW until ready to serve. In my slow cooker about 1 hour of holding time works best. Makes 4 servings.

Note: There is a lot of sausage in this recipe and it could easily serve 6 by making half again as much gravy, but the same amount of sausage.

Heat & Hold Scrambled Eggs

12	large eggs
1⅓	cups milk, divided
2	tablespoons flour
1	teaspoon salt
¼	teaspoon pepper
¼	cup butter (do not substitute)

Place eggs in a large mixing bowl and beat slightly. Add 1 cup milk and stir to blend. Combine the flour with the remaining ⅓ cup milk and whisk until smooth. Add to the egg mixture along with the salt and pepper.

Melt butter in a large 12-inch skillet. Add egg mixture and cook over medium heat, stirring frequently until eggs are cooked through, but still creamy. Do not overcook at this point; they will continue to cook somewhat when removed from the heat. Spoon into a sprayed slow cooker, cover and keep hot on the LOW setting. Makes 6 servings.

Note: The eggs will keep just perfect in my slow cooker for as long as an hour. If a very small amount of liquid collects in the bottom, this isn't a problem, just gently stir it back into the eggs.

Scrambled eggs, if allowed to stand any time at all, will become watery. This recipe will allow you more time, avoiding any last minute cooking, thus making life much easier if you are serving a lot of people.

Menu
*Heat & Hold Scrambled Eggs
Sausage Links
Fresh Fruit Salad
*Flaky Biscuits

Sausage & Apple Dish

A nice flavor and texture combination. Serve with an egg casserole, an omelet or scrambled eggs. Add toast or biscuits, some hot coffee and you have a full meal, whether served for breakfast or for dinner.

1	pound sausage links
6	medium apples
2	tablespoons fresh lemon juice
½	cup packed light brown sugar
¼	teaspoon salt (optional)

Brown sausage in a large skillet; cook through, but do not overcook. Drain on paper towels.

Meanwhile, core apples and cut each into eighths, but do not peel. Place in slow cooker and toss with the lemon juice and brown sugar. Add sausage and mix well. Cover and cook on LOW 7 to 8 hours or until apples are tender, but not mushy. Makes 6 servings.

Note: As liquid accumulates in the bottom of the slow cooker, the apples sitting in the liquid will cook faster than those on top. If possible, stir apples 2 or 3 times during the cooking time. If it isn't possible, don't worry about it, only a very few pieces may be a little too soft.

Southwestern Quiche

An easy quiche-like egg dish that forms somewhat of a soft crust on the bottom, thus eliminating the need for a pre-pared crust.

8	large eggs, lightly beaten
¼	cup flour
¼	cup butter, melted
2	cups (8-ounces) Monterey Jack cheese with peppers, shredded

Combine eggs, flour and butter. Whisk briskly to combine as much of the flour as possible. Fold in the cheese. Pour into a sprayed slow cooker and cook on HIGH 2 to 2½ hours or until custard is set. Makes 6 servings.

Chicken-Potato Chowder

3 chicken breast halves, skinned and boned
12 small red potatoes, unpeeled, cut into large cubes
2 cups frozen mixed vegetables, thawed
1 cup chopped onion
3 cans (14-ounces each) chicken broth
Salt and pepper to taste

This is a very filling soup, almost like a stew.

Cut chicken into bite-size pieces and quickly sauté until partially cooked; they should not be cooked through.

Add chicken along with potatoes, vegetables, onion and chicken broth to slow cooker. Cover and cook on HIGH 5½ to 6 hours or until potatoes are tender. Add salt and pepper to taste. Makes about 10 cups.

Note: Partially precooking the chicken will help to prevent so much scum from forming on the top. The chicken can sometimes overcook before the vegetables are tender. If desired, cook the chicken thoroughly, and add during the last half hour of cooking time.

Menu
Chicken-Potato Chowder
Sour Cream Muffins
Peach Melba Cups

Chili

To make chili dogs, simply place a hot dog in a bun on a plate, top with chili, shredded Cheddar cheese and diced onions.

2 pounds lean ground beef
1½ teaspoons salt
2½ teaspoons chili powder
1 teaspoon ground cumin
2 cans (14.5-ounces each) diced tomatoes, do not drain
2 cans (15-ounces each) kidney beans, drained

In large skillet, brown ground beef; drain. Add seasonings and cook 3 to 4 minutes. Add to slow cooker along with remaining ingredients. Stir in ¾ cup water. Cover and cook on LOW 7 to 8 hours. Makes 8 cups.

Ground Beef & Sweet Pepper Soup

Chili sauce gives this recipe a little extra zip. If you make the Company Cornish Hens on page 99, use the rest of the bottle to make this soup. Turn the bottle upside down and you will have almost a cup of sauce— plenty for this recipe.

1 pound lean ground beef
1 cup chopped onion
1 medium green pepper, cubed
1 cup chili sauce
1 can (14.5-ounces) diced tomatoes, with juice
1 cup uncooked long-grain rice

Brown ground beef, onion and peppers; drain and add to slow cooker along with remaining ingredients. Add 8 cups water. Cover and cook on Low 6 to 7 hours or until rice is tender. Makes 12 cups.

Note: It is necessary to at least partially cook the onion and green pepper along with the ground beef, otherwise the rice may be cooked through before the vegetables are tender.

Corn & Tomato Chowder

6   cups diced potatoes
3   cups frozen corn, thawed
2   cans (14.5-ounces each) diced tomatoes, with juice
1   cup chopped onion
   Salt and pepper to taste

Place ingredients in a slow cooker and add about 1½ cups water. Cover and cook on HIGH 6 to 7 hours or until vegetables are tender. Add salt and pepper to taste.

Note: In my slow cooker, it took over 14 hours to cook this soup on LOW. If you have the time, go ahead and cook on LOW, otherwise you can save a lot of time by cooking on HIGH.

Navy Bean Soup

1   package (16-ounces) dried small white beans
1   cup finely chopped onion
1   cup finely chopped celery
2   cups diced cooked ham
   Salt and pepper to taste

Clean beans as directed on package. Place in a 3-quart saucepan or stock pot. Add 8 cups water. Bring to a boil and cook about 3 minutes. Remove from heat and let stand one hour.

Place beans (and liquid) in slow cooker along with the onion, celery and ham. Cover and cook on LOW 13 to 14 hours (I know, that's a long time isn't it?). Season with salt and pepper. Make 10 cups.

Hint: Beans take a long time to cook in the slow cooker. I would suggest making the soup one day and reheating it when ready to serve.

Variation: To serve beans as a side dish, cook 12 hours (they will be a bit firmer than for soup; drain off most of the liquid.)

Beef Barley Soup

1	pound lean ground beef
1	cup finely chopped onion
½	cup pearl barley
2	medium carrots, shredded
8	cups well seasoned beef broth
1½	cups frozen peas, thawed

Brown ground beef and onion; drain. Place in a slow cooker and add remaining ingredients, except the peas. Cover and cook on LOW 4 to 5 hours or until barley is tender. Add peas last half hour of cooking time. Makes about 10 cups.

Chicken & Wild Rice Soup

1	can (10¾-ounces) condensed Cream of Chicken soup
6	cups chicken broth
1½	to 2 cups cubed cooked chicken
1	cup shredded carrots
1	package (6-ounces) Long-grain and Wild Rice mix with seasoning packet

Place soup in a sprayed slow cooker. Gradually stir in about 1 cup chicken broth. Add remaining broth and mix until smooth. Add remaining ingredients along with 2 cups water. Cover and cook on LOW 5 to 6 hours or until rice is tender. Do not overcook the rice. Makes about 12 cups.

Veggie Cheese Soup

1	can (15-ounces) creamed corn
4	cups potatoes, cubed
1½	cups carrots, cubed
¾	cup finely chopped onion
2	cans (14-ounces each) chicken broth
16	ounces process cheese spread, cubed

Place first 5 ingredients in slow cooker. Cover and cook on LOW 8 to 10 hours or until vegetables are tender. Add cheese; cover and cook until melted. Makes about 12 cups.

A nice blend of vegetables and cheese. Very good reheated.

Beef Stew

2	to 2½ pounds sirloin tip steak
1	cup chopped onion
3	cans (10¾-ounces each) condensed Cream of Chicken soup

Remove any fat on meat and cut into bite-size pieces. Place in a sprayed slow cooker. Sprinkle onion over top.

Place the soup in a medium bowl and stir until smooth. Pour over meat. Cover and cook on LOW 8 to 9 hours. Don't stir the mixture until it has cooked about 5 hours. Then quickly stir about once an hour after that, if possible. Makes 6 servings.

Tip: Rather than use the fork or knife test to check for doneness, use the taste test. Sometimes the meat will appear tender, but when you taste it, it may require more cooking.

This is an incredibly easy and delicious beef stew. The cream of chicken soup is quite unusual, but it turns into a very tasty beef flavored gravy. Serve over rice, noodles or mashed potatoes. The appearance for the first few hours is quite unappealing, but it does look nice at the end.

Sausage & Potato Chowder

A very filling main dish chowder. All you need for a complete meal is a delicious hearty bread and perhaps a nice fruit salad.

Variation: If desired, you can add any kind of sausage as a variation. You can also use ground beef and add salt and pepper or other seasonings for additional flavor.

1	package (12-ounces) sausage
1	cup chopped onion
4	cups potatoes, peeled, small cubes
1½	cups frozen corn, thawed
1	can (15-ounces) cream style corn
1	can (12-ounces) evaporated milk

Brown sausage and onion in a large skillet. Drain and place in slow cooker. Stir in remaining ingredients and cook on LOW 8 to 10 hours. Makes about 8 cups.

Note: If you want to speed up this recipe, cook on HIGH the entire time or on HIGH the last couple of hours. If chowder seems too thick, thin with a little milk the last hour of cooking time.

Potato Chowder

Note: The potatoes and onion take an unbelievably long time to cook in this recipe. To speed things up, you could cook on HIGH either at first or toward the end of the cooking time.

6	cups potatoes, peeled, small cubes
1	cup chopped onion
2	cans (14.5-ounces each) Italian style diced tomatoes
2	cups frozen corn, thawed
	Salt and pepper to taste

Place potatoes, onion, tomatoes, corn and 2 cups water in slow cooker. Cover and cook on LOW 10 to 12 hours or until potatoes are tender. Add salt and pepper to taste. Add additional water, if chowder is too thick. Makes about 10 cups.

Chili-No Beans

2	pounds lean ground beef
1	can (14.5-ounces) stewed tomatoes, drained
2	cans (8-ounces each) tomato sauce
1½	teaspoons salt
1	tablespoon chili, or to taste

Brown ground beef in a large skillet; drain. Add remaining ingredients and place in a sprayed slow cooker. Cover and cook on LOW 5 to 6 hours. Makes about 4 to 6 servings.

Ground Beef & Cheese Soup

1	pound lean ground beef
²/₃	cup chopped onion
2	cups potatoes, peeled, small cubes
1	cup frozen peas, thawed
1	cup frozen corn, thawed
16	ounces process cheese spread, cubed

Brown ground beef and onion in a large skillet; drain. Place in slow cooker. Add potatoes and 2 cups water. Cook on LOW 8 to 10 hours.

Add corn, peas, and cheese and cook about 20 to 30 minutes, or until heated through, stirring to blend.

There are some people who just don't like beans in their chili, but if you do, feel free to add them along with all the other ingredients. The chili can also be served over hot dogs topped with chopped onion and shredded cheese or over spaghetti. All you need is a green salad or a fresh vegetable tray and crackers or toasted hot rolls.

Everyone in my family loved this easy and delicious soup.

Note:*The soup may be quite thick when reheated. You can thin with milk or broth.*

Italian Sausage Soup

Note: *To reduce some of the fat, make soup ahead and chill. The fat will rise to the top and can easily be removed. To reduce fat even more, use ground beef and rinse thoroughly before adding to the soup.*

1	pound Italian sausage
1	small onion, halved crosswise and thinly sliced
1	small green pepper, cut into ½-inch cubes
1	can (14.5-ounces) diced tomatoes with juice
1	can (15-ounces) garbanzo beans, drained
2	cans (14-ounces each) beef broth

Brown the sausage, onion and green pepper; drain. Pour into a slow cooker along with remaining ingredients. Cover and cook on LOW 7 to 8 hours. Makes 7 cups.

Busy Day Potato Chowder

16	ounces frozen O'Brien hash browns, thawed
¼	cup chopped onion
1	can (15-ounces) whole corn, undrained
1	can (15-ounces) creamed corn
1	can (12-ounces) evaporated milk
½	teaspoon salt

Combine ingredients in slow cooker, cover and cook on LOW 7 to 8 hours. Makes 7 cups.

Ground Beef & Vegetable Soup

1	pound lean ground beef
½	cup chopped onion
2	cans (14.5-ounces each) Italian stewed tomatoes
2	cups frozen peas and carrots, thawed
	Salt and pepper to taste

Brown ground beef and onion; drain. Add to slow cooker along with remaining ingredients and 2½ cups water. Cover and cook on LOW 3 to 4 hours or until heated through. Makes about 12 cups.

Variation: The last 10 minutes of cooking time, add 2 cups cooked egg noodles or elbow macaroni, thus extending the recipe to feed another person or two.

Onion Soup

10	cups thinly sliced yellow onions
½	cup butter
2	cans (10.5-ounces each) condensed beef broth
1¹/₃	cups dry white wine
	French bread slices
	Shredded Mozzarella cheese

Melt butter in a large deep skillet or saucepan. Add onions and cook until soft, but not limp. Place in a slow cooker. Add beef broth, wine and 1¹/₃ cups water. Cover and cook on LOW 3 to 4 hours or until onion is tender. Makes about 9 cups.

Lightly toast bread on both sides. Sprinkle with Mozzarella cheese and broil until melted. Place on bowls of hot soup and serve.

One of my favorite meals: Onion soup, toasted cheese bread, tossed salad and Angel Food Cake with fresh fruit or lemon sauce on page 192.

Cheesy Zucchini & Potato Soup

Note: If desired, after adding the cheese, you can cook on LOW, until cheese has melted. This does make a lot, so you will need a large pot, a 5 to 6 quart size works great.

32	ounce package frozen hash browns, thawed
3	small zucchini, thinly sliced and halved
1	cup chopped onion
4	to 5 cups chicken broth or enough to cover
2	cups whipping cream
16	ounces process cheese spread, cubed

Place potatoes, zucchini and onion in a sprayed slow cooker. Add chicken broth to cover. Cover and cook on LOW 5 to 6 hours or until vegetables are tender.

Add whipping cream and cheese. Cover and cook on HIGH 2 to 2½ hours or until cheese has melted. Makes about 3 quarts.

Ground Beef & Corn Chowder

1	pound lean ground beef
½	cup chopped onion
1	can (15-ounces) white beans, drained
2	cups frozen mixed vegetables, thawed
1	can (15-ounces) tomato sauce
⅔	cup medium hot salsa

Brown ground beef and onion; drain and add to slow cooker. Add remaining ingredients along with 2 to 3 cups of water, or to a soup consistency. Cover and cook on LOW 7 to 8 hours. Makes about 10 cups.

Easy Family Soup

1   pound lean ground beef
1   cup chopped onion
1   can (10-ounces) Tomatoes and Green Chilies
2   cans (10¾-ounces each) condensed Minestrone soup

Brown ground beef and onion; drain. Spoon into a slow cooker. Add remaining ingredients along with 2 cups water. Cover and cook on LOW 3 to 4 hours or until heated through. Makes 7 cups.

We did a lot of camping when my children were small. With this soup, it was easy to have all the ingredients on hand.

Ground Beef & Cabbage Soup

1   pound lean ground beef
1   cup chopped onion
2   cans (14.5-ounces each) diced stewed tomatoes
½   of a small head of cabbage, thinly sliced
      Salt and pepper to taste

Brown ground beef and onion; drain and place in slow cooker. Add tomatoes and cabbage and enough water to cover, or to a soup consistency. Cover and cook on LOW 7 to 8 hours or until cabbage is tender. Add salt and pepper to taste. Makes 10 cups.

Even those of us who don't particularly like cooked cabbage enjoy it in a good soup recipe.

Asparagus Cheese Soup

This recipe is too good to reserve just for special occasions, so treat your family like company and serve in your prettiest soup bowls.

Tip: The soup can be made ahead and reheated and kept warm in the slow cooker. Or, reheat in a saucepan, stirring frequently until any small pieces of cheese are melted.

8   ounces fresh asparagus, trimmed, cut into 1-inch pieces

½   cup butter

¼   cup flour

2   cans (14-ounces each) chicken broth

   Pepper to taste

8   ounces Brie cheese, white rind removed, cubed

In a large saucepan, melt butter and cook asparagus until tender. Stir in flour and cook about 2 minutes. Gradually stir in the broth, mixing until smooth. Add pepper to taste. Bring to a boil, reduce heat and cook on medium-low heat 15 minutes. Blend half the soup at a time in a blender, watching carefully as soup is very hot. Also, make sure the lid is on tight.

Pour mixture into a sprayed slow cooker along with the Brie. Cover and cook on LOW 1 to 1½ hours or until cheese has melted. Soup can be served at this time or kept warm in the slow cooker a few minutes longer. Makes about 5 servings.

Process Cheese Spread

Most of us know this product under the more familiar names of Velveeta or American process cheese spread. They are most often found in 1, 3, and 5 pound boxes. Either brand will work in this cookbook, but you will notice a difference in the consistency. American cheese is firmer than Velveeta cheese and can be shredded. They have about the same melting qualities, and in most dishes I doubt you could taste the difference.

Ground Beef Stew

1 pound lean ground beef
1 cup chopped onion
1 cup frozen corn, thawed
1 can (15-ounces) chili beans Mexican style
1 can (14.5-ounces) diced stewed tomatoes
1 can (10¾-ounces) condensed Minestrone soup

Brown ground beef and onion; drain. Place in a slow cooker. Add remaining ingredients along with 2 cups water. Cover and cook on LOW 3 to 5 hours. Makes about 9 cups.

Make ahead and store in the refrigerator for those days when you have only a few minutes to prepare a meal.

Beef & Potato Stew

1 pound stew meat, cut into bite-size pieces
10 small red potatoes, halved (do not peel)
5 medium carrots, cut into 1-inch pieces
1 can (10¾-ounces) condensed Cream of Mushroom soup
1 can (10¾-ounces) condensed French Onion soup
⅓ cup red wine

Place meat, potatoes and carrots in slow cooker. Combine soups and wine and add to pot. Cover and cook on HIGH 8 to 10 hours or until meat is tender and vegetables are cooked through. Makes 4 large servings.

Variation: Use a thick cut of sirloin tip steak, cubed, for a more tender and flavorful stew meat.

Long slow cooking sometimes leaves the liquid in the pot looking rather bland. This recipe is enhanced by spooning into serving dishes and sprinkling with chopped parsley.

Southwestern Ground Beef Soup

This soup is really good but also really spicy. If you think it might be too hot for you, substitute flavored stewed tomatoes for the tomatoes with green chilies. Serve with corn-bread muffins.

1   pound lean ground beef
1   cup chopped onion
2   cups frozen mixed vegetables, thawed
1   jar (28-ounces) spaghetti sauce
1   can (10-ounces) Tomatoes with Green Chilies

Brown ground beef and onion; drain and place in a slow cooker. Add remaining ingredients along with 3 cups water. Cover and cook on LOW 4 to 5 hours. Makes about 10 cups.

Taco Soup

If you enjoy a somewhat south-western flavor, you will enjoy this spicy soup. It makes a lot, so make sure you are using a 4½ to 5 quart slow cooker.

2   pounds lean ground beef
1   package (1.25-ounces) taco seasoning mix
1   can (15-ounces) chili beans, rinsed and drained
2   cans (14.5-ounces each) diced stewed tomatoes
1   can (4-ounces) chopped green chilies
2   cups frozen corn, thawed

Brown ground beef; drain and then stir in seasoning mix. Spoon into a slow cooker. Add remaining ingredients along with 4 cups water. Cover and cook on LOW 6 to 7 hours. Makes 12 cups.

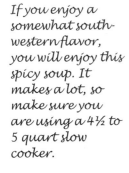

Meats & Seafood

Food Safety

There are two schools of thought on whether or not meats should initially be browned before cooking in a slow cooker. If you have the time, go ahead and brown the meat. The flavor will be locked in and slightly more intense although in some recipes you may not notice the difference. On the other hand, if you are putting a roast in the slow cooker before going to work, my customers are telling me they don't want to take the extra time it takes to brown the meat. I have kept browning to a minimum and if a recipe says to brown then I felt it was necessary. Other than ground beef, you will find that I have omitted that step in most of the recipes.

Frozen meat should always be thawed before placing in a slow cooker. The USDA maintains that it takes too long for frozen meat to reach a safe cooking temperature if placed in the slow cooker.

Beef

The nice thing about cooking meats in a slow cooker is that you don't have to use expensive cuts. In fact, cheaper cuts with a marble of fat are much more flavorful and tender.

In most cases, it isn't necessary to brown the meat before cooking, but you should trim any excess fat. Since liquids don't evaporate in slow cooking, you will have more liquid than when you started. The rich meaty flavor makes for great sauces and gravies.

Due to a lot of variables when slow cooking, you will see a wide range of cooking times. With some meats, an hour or two doesn't make a difference, with others you may come home to over-cooked meat. Regardless of what some books tell you, it is possible to cook meat too long.

Always check meat after the minimum cooking time suggested in the recipe.

Beef Rolls

A good family dish; nothing fancy, but very tasty. Serve with mashed potatoes.

Note: *Meat will shrink quite a bit; serving sizes should not be cut smaller unless you have a very small appetite.*

2	pounds top round steak
¼	cup Dijon mustard
1	medium onion, cut into slivers
3	cups beef broth
⅓	cup flour
	Seasoning salt

Cut meat into 4 serving size pieces. (See Note) Pound to ¼-inch thickness. Spread with mustard and scatter onion over top. Roll up and secure with toothpicks. Place in a slow cooker, cover and cook on LOW 8 to 9 hours or until meat is tender.

Combine flour with ½ cup water, mixing until smooth. Add to liquid and cook on HIGH 20 to 30 minutes or until thickened. Season to taste with seasoning salt. Makes 4 servings.

Swiss Steak

2½	to 3 pound round steak
1	cup chopped onion
1	can (14.5-ounces) diced tomatoes
½	green or red pepper, cubed
1	teaspoon salt
½	teaspoon Worcestershire sauce

Trim meat and cut into 6 serving size pieces. Place in slow cooker and top with remaining ingredients. Cover and cook on LOW 8 to 10 hours or until meat is tender.

Barbecue Beef Sandwiches

2½   to 3 pound beef chuck roast
¾   cup barbecue sauce, plus sauce for sandwiches
1   cup chopped onion

Trim roast of fat and place in slow cooker. Add barbecue sauce and onion. Cover and cook on LOW 10 to 12 hours or until meat is very tender. Shred meat using two forks. Serve on hamburger buns, using additional barbecue sauce, if desired. Makes about 8 sandwiches.

Note: If sandwiches are not to be served right away, place meat in a container and cover with some of the sauce from the slow cooker. Cover and chill until ready to use. Reheat and serve with additional barbecue sauce.

French Dip Sandwiches with Au Jus

1   3½ pound beef bottom round roast
2   medium onions, sliced
½   cup dry white wine
1   package (1.1-ounce) Au Jus mix
2   cups beef broth
    French or Hoagie rolls

Remove the top layer of fat on the roast. Place onion in bottom of slow cooker; add roast. Combine wine, Au Jus mix and broth; pour over meat. Cover and cook on LOW 9 to 10 hours or until meat is tender. Slice the meat for sandwiches. Remove broth from pot (discard onions) and strain. Serve in small bowls for dipping. Makes about 6 to 8 sandwiches.

Sandwich meat and Au Jus all in one pot. All you have to do later is heat the rolls.

Note: If I am home, I like to turn the meat over about half way through the cooking time. All this does is add color to the top half of the roast. Otherwise, don't worry about it.

Sirloin Tip Roast

4 to 4½ pound sirloin tip roast
1 teaspoon salt
1 cup chopped onion
½ cup red wine or beef broth
1 jar (14-ounces) spaghetti sauce with mushrooms

Trim roast of surface fat and the silver skin (causes meat to distort). Place in slow cooker and sprinkle with salt. Sprinkle onion over top.

Combine wine and spaghetti sauce and pour over meat. Cover and cook on LOW desired amount of time (see box below).

Sirloin Tip Roast

If you like your roast medium-rare and nice neat slices, cook meat to 140°. If you have my favorite meat thermometer, the one with the long cord and the timer, insert cord in meat at beginning of cooking time and set the thermometer to go off at 140°. Otherwise cook on LOW 10 to 12 hours or until meat is tender.

Note: *After reaching 150° to 160°, the meat will go from tender to very tough. The long slow cooking will take care of that, producing very tender meat.*

Family Pot Roast

5	pound rump roast
12	small new potatoes
6	carrots
1	large onion
1	teaspoon seasoning salt

Place half the potatoes in slow cooker. Cut carrots into 2-inch pieces and onion into wedges; place half over potatoes. Add roast and arrange remaining vegetables around meat. Add 1 cup water. Sprinkle with salt.Cover and cook on LOW 10 to 12 hours. If you happen to be at home, half way through cooking time, push the vegetables down into the broth. Makes 6 to 8 servings.

Ten to twelve hours is a long time to cook. You may want to do part of the cooking on HIGH.

Lemon Pepper Roast

1	2½ to 3 pound chuck roast
½	teaspoon seasoning salt
½	teaspoon lemon pepper
¼	teaspoon paprika
1	cup beef broth

Sprinkle meat with the combined mixture of salt, pepper and paprika. Place in slow cooker. Add beef broth. Cover and cook on HIGH about 4½ to 5 hours or until meat is tender. Makes 4 servings.

Note: Recipe can be cooked on LOW, but allow about 9 to 10 hours cooking time.

Corned Beef Brisket

This is one of the few recipes in the cookbook that require you to brown the meat first. The brisket is also cooked at a higher temperature. You can choose to cook it at a lower temperature, but it seems to take forever.

1   3 pound corned beef brisket
Seasoning salt
1   onion, coarsely chopped
3   carrots, coarsely chopped
3   plum tomatoes, chopped
1   cup beef broth

Sprinkle both sides of brisket generously with seasoning salt. Brown, fat side down, in a large skillet. Turn and brown other side.

Meanwhile, place vegetables in slow cooker. Place meat on top and add the beef broth. Cover and cook on HIGH 6 to 7 hours or until meat is tender. Thinly slice across the grain to serve. Makes about 6 servings.

Spicy Pot Roast

Leftovers: Shred meat and toss with barbecue sauce; heat and serve on hamburger buns. Or, add shredded meat to your favorite vegetable soup.

1   4 to 4½ pound beef chuck shoulder roast
¾   teaspoon garlic salt
¾   teaspoon pepper
2   teaspoons paprika
¼   teaspoon dry mustard

Rinse roast and pat dry. Combine remaining ingredients and rub over meat, coating all sides. Place roast in slow cooker. Add ½ cup water. Cover and cook on LOW 10 to 12 hours. Check after 10 hours of cooking time. Makes 6 to 8 servings.

Easy Beef Dinner

2   to 2½ pound round steak
4   medium potatoes, peeled and halved
4   carrots, cut crosswise into fourths
1   can (10¾-ounces) condensed French Onion soup

Trim fat from meat and cut into serving size pieces.

Place potatoes and carrots in slow cooker. Arrange meat over the vegetables. Pour soup over meat. Cover and cook on LOW 7 to 8 hours or until meat and vegetables are tender. Makes 4 to 5 servings.

Beef Stroganoff

1½   pound sirloin tip steak
1   cup chopped onion
1   can (14-ounces) beef broth
¼   teaspoon salt
¼   teaspoon pepper
1   cup sour cream

Cut meat crosswise into slightly less than ¼-inch slices. If slices are too long, cut in half. Place meat, onion, broth, salt and pepper in slow cooker. Cover and cook on HIGH 3½ to 4 hours or until meat is tender. Watch carefully last half hour of cooking time.

Add sour cream and stir until blended. Continue to cook until just heated through. Makes 4 servings.

If there is a lot of liquid, and the sour cream doesn't thicken it enough, rather than add more sour cream, add 4 tablespoons cornstarch mixed with 3 tablespoons water and heat until thickened. Serve over rice or noodles.

Ground beef can be used in so many different ways in a slow cooker. It is almost always browned first before mixing with remaining ingredients. Uncooked ground beef such as in a meatloaf, for safety reasons, should be cooked to at least 160°. Ground beef can be overcooked in a slow cooker. It takes on a somewhat grainy texture that is still tender, but rather unappealing. In addition to these recipes, why not adapt some of your favorite family recipes to slow cooking.

Cranberry Meatballs

Serve with pasta or a rice pilaf. To serve as an appetizer, make meatballs somewhat smaller and serve with toothpicks.

2   pounds lean ground beef
½   cup milk
1   large egg, lightly beaten
2   slices white bread, crumbled
1   can (16-ounces) whole cranberry sauce
1   bottle (12-ounces) chili sauce

Place ground beef in a large mixing bowl. Combine milk, egg and bread and add to meat. Combine until well mixed. Shape into walnut size balls and place on a large pan with 1-inch sides. They can be placed close together, but not touching. Bake at 425° for 12 to 15 minutes or until just lightly browned. Drain on paper towels. Place in a sprayed slow cooker.

Combine cranberry sauce and chili sauce; pour over meatballs. Cover and cook on LOW 3 to 4 hours or until heated through and sauce has thickened. Makes 40 meatballs. Makes about 6 servings.

Stuffed Green Peppers

1½ pounds lean ground beef
1¼ cups chopped onion
1 teaspoon salt
½ cup cooked long-grain rice
4 medium green peppers
1 can (8-ounces) tomato sauce

In a large skillet, brown ground beef and onion; drain. Add salt and rice and mix well.

Meanwhile, cut top off the green peppers and remove seeds. Place in slow cooker. Fill with ground beef mixture, spooning remaining meat around the peppers. Pour tomato sauce over top. Cover and cook on LOW 4 to 5 hours or until peppers are tender when pierced with a fork. Makes 4 to 6 servings.

Menu

*Sirloin Tip Roast
Mashed Potatoes
Green Beans
*Biscuit Muffins
*Peach & Raspberry Dessert

Mini Meatloaf for Two

This mini-loaf will make two generous servings or a little leftover for a sandwich.

1   pound lean ground beef
½   cup milk
1   cup soft bread crumbs
1   cup ketchup
3   tablespoons packed light brown sugar
2   tablespoons apple cider vinegar

Place ground beef in a medium mixing bowl. Combine milk and bread crumbs. Add to ground beef and gently mix to combine. Place in a sprayed slow cooker and form into a two-inch thick round.

Combine remaining ingredients and pour over top. Cover and cook on LOW 3½ to 4 hours or until meat registers 160°. Makes 2 to 4 servings.

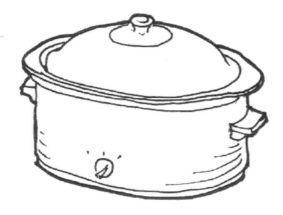

Mushroom Meatballs

2   pounds lean ground beef
4   large eggs, lightly beaten
½   teaspoon pepper
½   cup soft bread crumbs
²/₃ cup freshly grated Parmesan cheese
2   cans (10¾-ounces each) condensed Cream of
    Mushroom soup

Combine first five ingredients in a large bowl. Make 16 meatballs and place in a shallow baking pan. Bake at 425° for about 15 minutes or until meatballs are browned. Place in a sprayed slow cooker.

Combine soup with ½ cup water, mixing until smooth. Pour over meatballs. Cover and cook on LOW 5 to 6 hours. Makes 4 to 6 servings.

Ground Beef and Rice Dish

1   pound lean ground beef
1   cup frozen corn, thawed
1   can (14.5-ounces) stewed tomatoes, with juice
1   box (6-ounces) Long-grain and Wild Rice mix
    with seasoning packet

Brown ground beef in a large skillet; drain. Stir in the corn, tomatoes, rice mix and seasoning packet. Pour into a sprayed slow cooker and add 2½ cups water. Cover and cook on LOW 4 to 4½ hours or until liquid is absorbed and rice is tender. Taste for seasoning. You may want to add a little salt or pepper. Makes 6 servings.

Ground Beef Stroganoff

Stroganoff is always good served over hot buttered noodles or rice. Add a green vegetable or salad and toasted French bread or rolls. And, of course, a yummy dessert or maybe cookies and ice cream.

2	pounds lean ground beef
1½	cups chopped onion
1	can (4-ounces) sliced mushrooms, drained
1	cup beef broth
1	cup sour cream
¼	cup flour

Brown ground beef and onion in a large skillet; drain and place in a slow cooker along with the mushrooms.

Heat beef broth until hot. Add sour cream and mix until blended. Stir in the flour until smooth. Add to ingredients in slow cooker. Cover and cook on LOW 4 to 5 hours to heat through and blend flavors. Makes about 8 servings.

Note: If you don't have a well seasoned beef broth, you may need to add a little salt and pepper to taste.

Southwestern Beef & Beans

Very little fuss, just put the ingredients in the slow cooker and let it cook for several hours. Serve with corn bread or biscuits.

1	pound lean ground beef
¾	cup chopped onion
½	cup diced green pepper
1	can (14.5-ounces) diced Tomatoes with Green Chilies
1	can (15-ounces) black beans, drained

Brown ground beef, onion and green pepper; drain and place in a slow cooker along with remaining ingredients. Cover and cook on LOW 6½ to 7 hours. Makes 4 to 6 servings.

Chili Beef Dish

1½	pounds lean ground beef
1½	cups chopped onion
3	large plum tomatoes, diced
2	cans (15-ounces each) chili with beans

In a large skillet, brown ground beef and onion; drain and place in slow cooker. Stir in tomatoes and chili. Cover and cook on LOW 4 to 5 hours. Makes about 8 servings.

If you can find it in your area, my favorite brand of chili for this recipe is Cattle Drive®. It is a little bit sweet and a little bit spicy and packs a lot of flavor.

Ground Beef & Squash

1	pound lean ground beef
1	cup chopped onion
1	small green pepper, cubed
1	teaspoon salt
1	cup (4-ounces) Cheddar cheese, shredded
2	yellow crookneck squash, about 8-ounces each

Lightly brown the ground beef and onion in a large skillet. Add green pepper and cook until crisp tender; drain. Sprinkle with salt and half the cheese.

Cut squash in half lengthwise and scoop out the center. Place in a slow cooker and fill with the meat mixture. Spoon extra meat around squash. Cover and cook on LOW 3½ to 4 hours or until squash is just tender. Sprinkle with remaining cheese, cover and cook until melted, about 5 minutes. Makes 4 servings.

We all need economical recipes that are kind to our budget in our recipe files. This recipe works best if you have an oval shaped slow cooker.

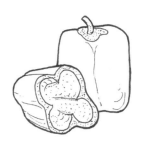

Meat Sauce

*E*veryone needs a good basic meat sauce recipe. This one makes a lot of sauce that can be divided into portions and frozen. This recipe is very good as is, but if desired, you can add your favorite seasonings either during the cooking time or at the end.

4	pounds lean ground beef
2	cups coarsely chopped onion
4	large garlic cloves, finely chopped
4	teaspoons salt
1¼	teaspoons pepper
3	cans (28-ounces each) whole tomatoes with juice, coarsely chopped

Brown ground beef, onion and garlic in a large stock pot or Dutch oven until meat is no longer pink; drain. Place in a 5 to 6 quart slow cooker. Add salt and pepper. Add the tomatoes; cover and cook on LOW 8 to 9 hours. Check for seasoning, adding more salt and pepper to taste. Makes 16 cups sauce.

The meat sauce can be used for:

Spaghetti	Taco Salads	Lasagna	Baked Potato Topping
Chili	Soups	Casseroles	Stuffed Peppers

If you are making spaghetti and find the sauce doesn't stick to the pasta like you want it to, there is a remedy. Reheat the sauce on top of the stove and cook to a somewhat thicker consistency.

Linda's Beef Curry Casserole

1   pound lean ground beef
1   cup uncooked long-grain rice
1   teaspoon salt
1   teaspoon curry powder
1   can (8-ounces) crushed pineapple, with juice
½   cup raisins

Brown ground beef in large skillet; drain.

Meanwhile, place rice in a sprayed slow cooker. Add 2¼ cups water along with the salt, curry powder, pineapple and raisins. Add ground beef. Cover and cook on HIGH 2 to 3 hours. Watch carefully after 2 hours. In my slow cooker, 2½ hours is perfect. Makes 6 servings.

My daughter Linda, is a busy mom and makes this often for her family. The curry and fruit makes a delectable combination for a delicious family meal.

Easy Goulash

1   pound lean ground beef
½   cup chopped onion
1   can (15-ounces) dark kidney beans, drained
1   can (10½-ounces) vegetable soup

Brown ground beef and onion; drain off fat. Add remaining ingredients. Pour into a slow cooker and cook on LOW 3 to 3½ hours. Makes 6 servings.

Just everyday family fare, but tasty just the same.

Easy Ravioli Lasagna

What an easy way to make lasagna, but you do have to re-member not to thaw the ravioli before adding to the pot. I have used a lot of cheese in this recipe, but it really does make a difference. When dishing it up, everyone wants their share of the delicious, hot stringy cheese.

1½ pounds lean ground beef
1   cup diced onion
1   tablespoon packed light brown sugar
1   jar (28-ounces) spaghetti sauce with mushrooms
1   package (25-ounces) frozen cheese filled ravioli
5   cups (20-ounces) Mozzarella cheese, shredded

Brown ground beef and onion; drain thoroughly. Add brown sugar and spaghetti sauce and heat through.

Spoon a thin layer of sauce over bottom of a sprayed slow cooker. Add a single layer of frozen ravioli (do not thaw). Cover with half the remaining sauce, then half the cheese. Repeat layers (you will probably have a few ravioli left over). Cover and cook on HIGH 3 to 4 hours or until very hot and cheese has melted. Makes 8 to 10 servings.

Note: I made this in my 5 quart oval slow cooker. I wouldn't suggest anything smaller than a 3½ to 4 quart size. If you are using a round pot, depending on the size, you may have to make 3 layers instead of two, keeping in mind that the pasta should be a single layer deep each time you layer the ingredients.

Hamburger & Potato Dish

1½	pounds lean ground beef
1	cup chopped onion
1½	teaspoons salt
1	can (15-ounces) dark kidney beans, drained
1	can (14.5-ounces) diced tomatoes, with juice
4	cups frozen hash browns, partially thawed

Brown ground beef and onion in a 12-inch skillet; drain. Stir in the salt, beans and tomatoes. Place hash browns in a sprayed slow cooker. Top with ground beef mixture. Cover and cook on LOW 5 to 6 hours or until potatoes are tender. Makes 6 servings.

Serve with a variety of fresh raw vegetables and hot rolls.

Stroganoff Meatballs

1	can (14.5-ounces) beef broth
¼	cup flour
1	cup chopped onion
2	tablespoons butter, melted
30	precooked meatballs, fresh or frozen, thawed
1	cup sour cream

Combine beef broth and flour in slow cooker, whisking until smooth. Add onion, butter and meatballs. Cover and cook on LOW 4 to 5 hours.

Add sour cream and gently stir until blended. Cook, on HIGH, 30 minutes. Serve on rice or noodles. Makes 4 to 6 servings.

This recipe is only as good as the meatballs you use. There are very good ones you can purchase fresh or frozen and then there are those that aren't so good. You can make your own by forming 2 pounds ground beef into small balls and browning in oven.

Meatloaf Dijon

Serve with
mashed pota-
toes, green
beans, hot rolls
and Rustic Apple
Pie.

1½	pounds lean ground beef
1/3	cup crushed Saltine crackers
½	cup finely chopped onion
1/3	cup ketchup
1	tablespoon Dijon mustard
1	large egg, lightly beaten

Combine all ingredients until well mixed. Place in slow cooker and form into a round about the size of the bottom of the pot. Cook on LOW 5 to 6 hours. Temperature should reach no less than 160° F. Makes 6 servings.

Tamale Casserole

Anyone who likes
the flavor of
tamales will like
this very easy
casserole.

1	pound lean ground beef
1	cup chopped onion
1	can (14½-ounces) chunky tomatoes, drained
1	can (4-ounces) diced green chilies
8	(6-inch) soft corn tortillas
2	cups (8-ounces) Cheddar cheese, shredded

Brown ground beef and onion; drain. Add tomatoes and green chilies and heat through.

Tear 4 of the tortillas into bite-size pieces and place in a sprayed slow cooker. Add half the meat mixture; then sprinkle with half the cheese. Repeat layers, ending with cheese. Cover and cook on LOW 2 to 2½ hours or until heated through. Makes 4 generous servings.

Hamburger and Beans

1½   pounds lean ground beef
1½   cups chopped onion
1   can (14-ounces) whole tomatoes, drained
1   can (1-pound, 15-ounces) pork and beans
½   cup packed light brown sugar
½   cup ketchup

Brown ground beef and onion; drain. Place in slow cooker.

Cut tomatoes into small pieces. Add to pot. Stir in remaining ingredients. Cover and cook on LOW 6 to 7 hours. Makes about 10 servings.

Beef and Rice Casserole

1½   pounds lean ground beef
1½   cups chopped onion
1½   cups uncooked long-grain rice
1   can (10¾-ounces) condensed Cream of Celery soup
1   can (10¾-ounces) condensed Cream of Mushroom soup
1   teaspoon salt

Brown ground beef and onion; drain, and place in slow cooker. Add remaining ingredients along with 2 soup cans of water. Cover and cook on LOW 6 to 7 hours or until liquid is absorbed and rice is tender. Makes 8 servings.

Pasta Tip

Remember that pasta will continue cooking once in the slow cooker. To prevent overcooking, pasta should be slightly undercooked before adding to recipes in a slow cooker.

Pot Luck Casserole

Note: Undercook the pasta just slightly as it will continue to cook in the slow cooker.

Variation: Omit the sour cream and add 4 ounces mushrooms, sliced, to the ground beef and onion mixture.

8   ounces penne pasta
2   pounds lean ground beef
2   cups coarsely chopped onion
3   cups chunky spaghetti sauce
1½ cups sour cream
4   cups (16-ounces) Mozzarella cheese, shredded

Cook pasta according to package directions. Drain and rinse with cold water. Brown ground beef and onion; drain. Add spaghetti sauce and bring to a boil. Reduce heat and simmer about 5 minutes.

In a sprayed slow cooker, layer with half the pasta, meat, sour cream and cheese. Repeat layers, ending with the cheese. Cover and cook on LOW 4 to 4½ hours to heat through. Makes 8 to 10 servings.

Ground Beef Noodle Bake

Note: If you are going to be home, add the Cheddar cheese the last ½ hour of cooking time. If not, don't worry about it, it may not look as nice, but it will taste the same.

1   pound lean ground beef
3   cups chunky spaghetti sauce with mushrooms
6   ounces egg noodles
1   cup sour cream
1   cup small curd cottage cheese
1   cup (4-ounces) Cheddar cheese, shredded

Brown ground beef; drain. Add spaghetti sauce and cook until liquid is absorbed. Cook pasta according to package directions; drain and place in a sprayed slow cooker along with the sour cream and cottage cheese. Spread meat sauce over top. Sprinkle with cheese. Cover and cook on LOW 3 to 3½ hours to heat through. Makes 6 servings.

Spaghetti with Meatballs

4	pounds lean ground beef
1	package (0.7-ounces) Italian dressing mix
1	package (1½ cups) finely crushed Saltine crackers
2	large eggs, lightly beaten
6	cups spaghetti sauce with mushrooms

Combine first 4 ingredients in a large mixing bowl. Form into meatballs a little larger than the size of walnuts. Place in a large shallow roasting pan and bake at 425° for 18 to 20 minutes or until browned and cooked through.

Place in a sprayed slow cooker and add spaghetti sauce. Cover and cook on LOW 5 to 6 hours. Makes about 60 meatballs and about 12 servings.

Ways to Serve:

Serve over spaghetti and sprinkle with cheese.

Make meatball sandwiches served in Hoagie buns.

Serve over baked potatoes.

This is a very large recipe which is wonderful when serving a crowd or a large group of teenagers. There are times though, when you may not want this much spaghetti. Go ahead and make the meatballs and use desired amount for a spaghetti dinner. Divide and freeze the rest for another time. Or reduce the recipe by half.

Soft Taco Bean Casserole

This may look like a long recipe, but by listing each layer in order, it makes assembling much easier.

1½	pounds lean ground beef
2	cups chunky salsa, divided
5	(8-inch) flour tortillas
2	cups (8-ounces) Cheddar cheese, shredded
1	can (16-ounces) refried beans

Brown ground beef; drain. Add 1 cup of the salsa and cook over low heat about 5 to 6 minutes or until heated through.

In sprayed slow cooker, layer in this order:

Half the meat mixture

One tortilla

Half the cheese

One tortilla

Half the refried beans

One tortilla

Remaining meat mixture

One tortilla

Remaining refried beans

One tortilla

Remaining cheese

Then spoon the remaining 1 cup salsa over the cheese. Cover and cook on LOW 4 to 4½ hours or until very hot in the center. Makes 6 to 8 servings.

Beef Barley Dish

1	pound lean ground beef
1	cup chopped onion
1	can (14.5 ounces) diced Italian tomatoes, with juice
1½	cups frozen mixed vegetables, thawed
¾	cup pearl barley
1	teaspoon salt or to taste

Brown ground beef and onion; drain. Spoon into a sprayed slow cooker. Add remaining ingredients along with 2½ cups water. Cover and cook on LOW 5 to 6 hours or until barley is tender and liquid is absorbed. Makes 6 to 8 servings.

Chocked full of vegetables, this may be one way to get your children to eat them.

Ground Beef Pasta Bake

1	pound lean ground beef
1	cup chopped onion
1½	cups uncooked elbow macaroni
2	cans (14.5-ounces each) diced Italian stewed tomatoes with juice
1	can (15-ounces) white beans, drained
1	can (15-ounces) kidney beans, drained

Brown ground beef and onion; drain and place in a sprayed slow cooker.

Meanwhile, cook the pasta, drain and place in slow cooker. Add the stewed tomatoes and beans; cover and cook on LOW 2 hours or until heated through. Makes about 6 servings.

What a great way to stretch a pound of ground beef and feed a hungry family.

Note: If you don't have well-seasoned stewed tomatoes, you may want to add a little salt to taste.

Sweet-Sour Country-Style Ribs

Long cooking will cause the peppers to darken, but by adding them at the end they will retain their bright color. If desired, you can use both red and green peppers. Serve over rice.

3	to 4 pounds boneless country-style pork ribs
1	can (20-ounces) pineapple chunks, with juice
¼	cup white vinegar
½	cup packed light brown sugar
½	red or green pepper, cut into narrow strips
4	tablespoons cornstarch

Place ribs in slow cooker. Combine the pineapple and juice, vinegar and brown sugar. Pour over ribs. Cover and cook on LOW 6 to 7 hours or until meat is tender.

Remove meat and set aside. Pour pineapple mixture (be careful, pot is hot) into a medium saucepan. Add pepper strips. Combine cornstarch with 3 tablespoons cold water and add to saucepan. Cook over medium heat until thickened, stirring occasionally. Makes 6 servings.

Don't Peek

We are curious creatures and the temptation is always there to take a peek at what is cooking. Valuable heat is lost each time we lift the lid, extending the cooking time by about 20 minutes. That's how much time it can take to recover the heat that is lost. So, if the cooking time is important, try to keep peeking to an absolute minimum.

Pork Chops in Orange Sauce

4   loin-cut pork chops, 1-inch thick
Lemon pepper
1   teaspoon oil
1   large orange
¼   cup orange marmalade
½   cup ketchup

Sprinkle pork chops lightly with lemon pepper. Quickly brown in oil and place in slow cooker.

From the orange you will need ½ cup orange juice and 1 teaspoon orange zest. Combine with marmalade and ketchup and pour over pork chops. Cover and cook on LOW 6 to 8 hours or until meat is tender. Makes 4 servings.

One of my customers, Cal, made this recipe with the only keptchup he had on hand - his kid's green ketchup. He said the flavor was fine, but the color left something to be desired.

Menu

*Pork Chops in Orange Sauce
Rice Pilaf
Fresh Green Beans
*Apple Cinnamon Crisp

Ham & Salami Lasagna Rolls

This is one of the easiest lasagna recipes ever. Don't be intimidated by the rolling of the filled noodles; it is very easy.

Note: When placing the filled rolls in the slow cooker, the noodle side should be showing, not the filling side.

6   lasagna noodles
8   ounces Deli ham, diced
4   ounces salami, diced
4   cups (16-ounces) Mozzarella cheese, shredded
1   jar (26-ounces) tomato-basil spaghetti sauce

Cook pasta according to package directions, cooking until "almost" tender, but not quite. They will continue to cook in the slow cooker. Drain and rinse with cold water.

Lay the 6 noodles out on a bread board or counter. Combine ham, salami and half the cheese in a mixing bowl. Spoon mixture evenly over the noodles. (If you have any mixture left over, that's okay; you can sprinkle it over the rolls after placing them in the pot.) Roll each noodle.

Spoon three fourths of the spaghetti sauce in a sprayed slow cooker, place each roll, seam side down, over the sauce, making one layer. Sprinkle remaining meat mixture over rolls. Then sauce and cheese. Cover and cook on HIGH 3 to 4 hours or until very hot. I like to cook until the cheese browns around the edge. Makes 6 servings.

Note:You may want to cook 2 to 3 extra noodles just in case some of them break. Using plenty of water to cook them in will help eliminate this problem.

Baby Back Ribs for Two

½ to ¾ rack of baby back ribs
Salt and pepper

Rinse rack of ribs, pat dry and trim excess fat. Generously sprinkle both sides with salt and pepper using more seasoning than you normally would. Don't worry, some of it is cooked off, so it will not be too salty. Place, meaty side up, in a sprayed slow cooker. Do not add anything else. Cover and cook on LOW 7 to 8 hours or until browned and tender. Serves 2 (or maybe only one, they are that good).

Note: To make this recipe work, the size of the rack of ribs should be what you can fit in one layer on the bottom of the slow cooker. I tried increasing the recipe by standing the racks around the outside of the slow cooker, meaty side out, but they didn't brown. (If you want to cook more ribs, stand around edge of pot and cook about 7 hours on LOW or until almost tender. Then place on a baking pan and bake at 400° for 15 to 20 minutes or until browned and cooked through.) Makes 2 servings.

You won't believe these were cooked in a slow cooker. They are nicely browned and look like they came out of the oven or off the grill. This works best for 2 servings of ribs and in a large oval shaped slow cooker.

Barbecue Ribs

1½ racks of baby back ribs, about 20 ribs
Choice of barbecue sauce

Wash and trim ribs of excess fat. Cut into 2-rib sections. Brush both sides of ribs with barbecue sauce. Place as many ribs, meaty side out, as you can, around the pot. Place remaining ribs on the bottom, meaty side up. Cover and cook on LOW 8 to 9 hours or until tender. Makes 4 to 5 servings.

Ribs are moist, tender and delicious cooked in a slow cooker. You may want to brush additional sauce on the ribs just before serving or pass extra sauce at the table.

Broccoli Ham Casserole

I have to tell you this tastes a lot better than it looks, but it is a great way to use up that last bit of ham and broccoli you may have in the refrigerator.

1   can (10¾-ounces) condensed Cream of Mushroom soup
1   cup milk
1   cup diced ham
2   cups broccoli florettes
1   cup uncooked instant rice
8   ounces process cheese spread, cubed

Place soup in slow cooker and gradually whisk in the milk until smooth. Add remaining ingredients. Cover and cook on LOW 3½ to 4 hours. If possible, stir mixture half way through the cooking time. Makes 4 servings.

Pork Chop & Sweet Potato Bake

Note: Pork chops cook very well in a slow cooker, but they should be at least ¾ to 1-inch thick.

4   rib-cut pork chops, 1-inch thick
2   pounds sweet potatoes, about 3 medium
¼   cup packed light brown sugar
1   can (8-ounces) crushed pineapple with juice

Rinse pork chops and pat dry. Trim off the fat. Place in one layer in a sprayed slow cooker.

Peel sweet potatoes and cut crosswise into 1-inch slices. Add to slow cooker. Sprinkle with brown sugar. Add pineapple; cover and cook on LOW 7 to 8 hours or until pork chops and potatoes are tender. Makes 4 servings.

Sausage Pilaf

1   package (12-ounces) pork sausage
¾   cup thinly sliced celery
¼   cup slivered almonds
1   package (6-ounces) Long-grain and Wild Rice mix
    with seasoning packet
3   cups chicken broth

Sausage and rice makes a nice combination for lunch or a light dinner.

Brown sausage in medium skillet; drain. Add to slow cooker along with remaining ingredients. Cover and cook on LOW 5 to 5½ hours or until liquid is absorbed and rice is tender. Makes 4 servings.

Note: If rice is tender, but there is liquid still remaining in the pot, it is best to drain rather than continue cooking which may produce a soft mushy rice.

PORK

The fear of trichinosis was at one time associated with eating undercooked pork. This organism has been almost completely eliminated today, but in any case, is destroyed at an internal temperature of 137° which is well below the recommended finished cooking temperature of 150° to 165°.

There are times, no matter what you do, pork will be tough. And it may not be your fault. The single most important factor for fork tender pork is the age of the animal. The second, believe it or not, is the psychological state of the pig at the time it is slaughtered. If that little piggy went to market and it was tired, scared or shocked, its endocrine glands work overtime and alters the texture of the meat. No kidding! So now, if your pork is tough, you have an interesting story to tell.

Southwestern Strata

Strata type dishes can be assembled the night before and chilled until ready to cook. This recipe is no exception, but it works just as well if you want to omit that step and cook right away. Serve as a main dish for lunch, brunch, or dinner.

1	pound bulk sausage
1	loaf (16-ounces) French or Italian bread
2	cups chunky salsa
3	cups (12-ounces) Mozzarella cheese, shredded
6	large eggs
2	cups milk

Brown sausage in a medium skillet; drain off fat.

Cut bread into cubes (no need to remove the crust). Arrange half the bread cubes in a sprayed slow cooker. Spoon half the salsa over the bread. Top with half the sausage and then half the cheese. Repeat layers.

Combine eggs and milk and beat until thoroughly mixed. Pour over the cheese layer. Cover and cook on LOW 4 to 5 hours or until heated through. Makes 12 servings.

Baked Beans with Polish Sausage

A flavorful bean dish. Serve as a light main dish or as a side dish.

8	to 10 ounces Kielbasa, cubed or sliced
1	can (31-ounces) pork and beans
¼	cup finely chopped onion
2	tablespoons packed light brown sugar
2	teaspoons Dijon mustard
¼	cup ketchup

Combine ingredients in a sprayed slow cooker. Cover and cook on LOW 5 to 6 hours or until mixture has thickened slightly. Makes 4 to 6 servings.

Ham & Cheese Bake

    3   cups frozen hash browns, thawed
    1   cup (4-ounces) Swiss cheese, shredded
 1½   cups small cubed ham
    1   cup (4-ounces) Monterey Jack cheese with
        peppers, shredded
    4   large eggs, lightly beaten
    1   cup half and half

Place hash browns in a sprayed slow cooker. Sprinkle with Swiss cheese, then ham and then the Monterey Jack cheese. Combine eggs and half and half and mix well. Pour over potato mixture. Cover and cook on HIGH 4 to 4½ hours. Makes 6 servings.

Sausage & Wild Rice Casserole

    1   package (12-ounces) sausage
   ¾   cup sliced celery
    1   cup chopped onion
    1   package (6-ounces) Long-grain and Wild Rice mix
        with seasoning packet

Brown sausage, celery and onion in a large skillet; drain. Place in a slow cooker. Add rice and seasoning packet along with 2¼ cups water. Cover and cook on LOW 2½ to 3 hours or until liquid is absorbed and rice is tender. Makes 4 to 6 servings.

Baked Beans & Hot Dogs

Is there anyone who doesn't like baked beans? Well maybe, but perhaps this recipe will change their mind. Serve with cornbread muffins. Add a salad and then your favorite cake for dessert.

1	cup chopped onion
½	cup packed light brown sugar
3	tablespoons prepared mustard
6	slices bacon, cooked and crumbled
3	cans (28-ounces each) pork and beans
6	to 8 hot dogs

Place first 5 ingredients in a slow cooker.

Cut hot dogs into ¼-inch slices and add to beans. Cover and cook on LOW 7 to 8 hours. Makes 10 to 12 servings.

Variation: Omit the hot dogs and serve beans with hamburgers, ribs or fried chicken. Add coleslaw and corn on the cob and you'll have a meal I doubt anyone will want to turn down.

Note: The baked beans will be a little on the soupy side. If you would prefer them a little thicker, cook uncovered on HIGH the last hour of cooking time.

Italian Sausage Merlot

Nothing fancy here, but it does produce very flavorful sausage links. Slice and eat with Italian bread as a snack or for lunch. Or, cut into a small dice and add to a casserole, strata or soup.

3	tablespoons Currant jelly
1	cup Merlot or desired red wine
1	cup finely chopped onion
6	Italian sausages

In a slow cooker, whisk the jelly and wine until smooth. Add the onion and sausages and cook on HIGH 2 to 3 hours or until the sausages are cooked through. Makes 3 to 4 servings.

Pork Roast

1   2½ to 3 pound Boston pork butt roast
Salt and pepper
Garlic salt
Paprika

Place roast in a slow cooker (no liquid). Sprinkle with remaining ingredients. Cover and cook on LOW 10 to 12 hours or until meat is tender enough to shred with a fork. Makes 4 to 6 servings.

Pork & Wild Rice Casserole

4   to 6 boneless pork chops, 1 to 1½-inches thick
1   can (10¾-ounces) condensed Cream of
     Chicken soup
1   can (10¾-ounces) condensed Cream of
     Mushroom soup
1   can (10¾-ounces) condensed Cream of
     Celery soup
1   box (6-ounces) Long grain and Wild Rice mix
     with seasoning packet

Remove excess fat from pork chops. Place soups in sprayed slow cooker. Add ¼ cup water. Stir in rice, then add pork chops, pushing down into the soup until coated. Cover and cook on LOW 7 to 8 hours or until pork is tender and liquid is absorbed. Makes 4 to 6 servings.

Note: Whether you use the seasoning mix from the rice or not is up to you. I found it to be quite salty in this recipe. If you would like a little crunch, add slivered almonds or chopped water chestnuts.

A Boston pork butt roast is marbled with a small amount of fat that makes for a very tender and moist cut of meat. Serve like a pot roast, or cool slightly, and shred the meat with a fork. Toss with your favorite barbecue sauce and serve on hamburger buns with shredded cabbage.

Sausage Rice Casserole

Variations of this recipe have been around for as long as I can remember. Making it in the slow cooker will free you to do other things.

1½ pounds sausage
2 cups chopped celery
1 cup chopped onion
¼ cup slivered almonds
2 packages (4.2-ounces) Chicken Noodle Soup mix
1 cup uncooked long-grain rice

In large skillet, brown sausage until almost cooked through. Add celery and onion and cook until almost tender; drain. Place in slow cooker. Add remaining ingredients along with 4 cups of water. Cover and cook on LOW 4 to 4½ hours or until liquid is absorbed and rice is tender. Makes 8 to 10 servings.

Pork Chops with Mushroom Sauce

This really is one of those quick, put it in a pot and forget it recipes. For a real comfort meal, serve with mashed potatoes, green beans and hot dinner rolls. Apple pie would really round out the meal.

4 pork chops, ¾ to 1-inch thick
1 can (10¾-ounces) condensed Mushroom with Roasted Garlic soup

Trim fat from pork chops. Place in a slow cooker; stir soup and pour over meat. Cover and cook on LOW 7 to 8 hours. Stir sauce and serve over pork chops. Makes 4 servings.

Note: In my slow cooker, 7 hours is just about right, after that the pork chops start to fall apart, but that is also the way a lot of people like them.

Kielbasa & Sauerkraut

8   small red potatoes, unpeeled and cut into small chunks
1   medium onion, thinly sliced
2   cans (14-ounces each) sauerkraut, drained well
1¼   cups chicken broth
½   teaspoon caraway seeds
1   to 1½ pounds kielbasa

Place first 5 ingredients in a slow cooker in order listed. Cut kielbasa diagonally into 2½ to 3-inch slices. Arrange over sauerkraut. Cover and cook on LOW 7 to 8 hours. Check potatoes to make sure they are tender. Makes 4 to 6 servings.

For a full meal, all you need is a green vegetable or two and your favorite hot bread. If you aren't rushed for time, a green salad would also be nice.

Broccoli Potato Pork Chops

4   pork chops, ¾ to 1-inch thick
4   medium potatoes, cut into ¼-inch slices
½   cup milk
1   can (10¾-ounces) condensed Broccoli Cheese soup

Trim pork chops of excess fat. Place potatoes in a sprayed slow cooker. Arrange pork chops over top. Combine milk and soup, mixing until smooth. Pour over pork chops. Cover and cook on LOW 7 to 8 hours or until meat and potatoes are tender. Makes 4 servings.

Note: If you are using rib-cut pork chops and they won't quite fit in one layer, the long narrow end of the bone often has a break in it and can easily be removed.

Simple, easy and packed full of flavor. The broccoli is that added flavor that makes it interesting. Do not overcook the potatoes or they will turn dark.

Chili Dog Tortillas

Note: *If you can't find a 19-ounce can of chili, use the next larger size. In fact, a little more chili just makes it that much better. This recipe would also work well, if you need more time, by cooking it on LOW for about 3 to 4 hours.*

4   (8-inch) flour tortillas, warmed
1   can (19-ounces) Chili with beans
4   hot dogs
½   cup (2-ounces) Cheddar cheese, shredded

Spread each tortilla with ¼ cup chili. Place a hot dog toward one side and roll up. Place seam-side down, in a sprayed slow cooker. Spoon remaining chili over top. Sprinkle with cheese. Cover and cook on HIGH 2 hours or until heated through. Makes 4 servings.

Swiss Hot Dogs & Sauerkraut

1   jar (32-ounces) sauerkraut, drained well
1½   teaspoons caraway seeds
8   hot dogs
1½   cups (6-ounces) Swiss cheese, shredded

Place sauerkraut in a sprayed slow cooker. Add caraway seeds and toss to mix. Add hot dogs and sprinkle with cheese. Cover and cook on LOW 3½ to 4 hours or until heated through. Makes 4 servings.

Pork Tenderloin with Mushroom Gravy

2   pork tenderloins (total weight 2 to 2½ pounds)
1   can (10¾-ounces) condensed Cream of
      Mushroom soup
1   can (10¾-ounces) condensed Golden
      Mushroom soup
1   can (10¾-ounces) condensed French Onion soup

Trim pork of excess fat and silver skin. Place in a sprayed slow cooker. Combine all three soups until blended. Pour over meat. Cover and cook on LOW 6 to 7 hours or until meat is tender. Makes 4 to 6 servings.

You can have this recipe in the pot and cooking in less than 10 minutes. Serve the delicious meat and sauce over mashed potatoes or noodles.

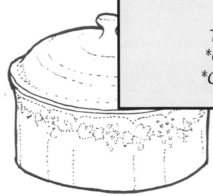

Menu

*Pork Tenderloin with Mushroom Gravy
Mashed Potatoes
Carrots
Tossed Green Salad
*Quick Bran Muffins
*Chocolate Chip Cake

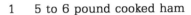
Slow Cooked Ham

A great way to easily cook a ham.

Note: *On Easter, I had a ham that was too large for the slow cooker. It would fit inside, but I couldn't use the lid. I covered the top of the ham with heavy-duty foil, and pressed the foil tightly around the rim of the slow cooker. It worked beautifully and freed up my oven for other dishes.*

1	5 to 6 pound cooked ham
½	cup apricot preserves

Place ham, cut side down in slow cooker. Cover and cook on LOW 4 to 5 hours or until meat thermometer reaches 120°. Brush with apricot preserves, cover and cook on HIGH 20 to 30 minutes or until meat thermometer reaches 140°.

Ham & Pasta Casserole

16	ounces rotini or penne pasta
½	cup butter, divided
3	tablespoons flour
1⅓	cups milk
2	cups (8-ounces) cubed ham
¾	cup freshly grated Parmesan cheese, divided

Cook pasta according to package directions, but remove pasta before it reaches the al dente stage. Drain and rinse with hot water. Return to pan and keep hot.

Meanwhile, melt 2 tablespoons of the butter in a medium saucepan. Add flour and whisk until smooth; cook about 1 minute, stirring frequently. Remove from heat and add milk, whisking until smooth. Return to heat and cook until thickened, stirring frequently. Add the remaining butter. Stir in ½ cup of the Parmesan cheese. Place pasta in a sprayed slow cooker. Add ham and cream sauce and quickly stir until blended. Cover and cook on LOW 3 to 3½ hours or until heated through. Makes 6 to 8 servings.

Barbecue Pork Chops

4   pork chops, about ¾-inch thick
¾   cup barbecue sauce, divided

Trim fat from meat and pat dry. Place in one layer in a sprayed slow cooker. Spoon ½ cup of the barbecue sauce over the top. Cover and cook on LOW 7 to 8 hours or until meat is tender. During last hour of cooking time, spread remaining sauce over the pork chops, or serve the sauce on the side. Makes 4 servings.

Everyone needs a very simple recipe to make on those hectic days when you don't know if you are coming or going. This recipe is simple but good.

Barbecue Country Style Ribs

2   to 2½ pounds country style pork ribs with bone
½   cup packed light brown sugar
1   cup ketchup
2   tablespoons Worcestershire sauce
1   tablespoon prepared mustard
¼   cup lemon juice

Place pork ribs in a sprayed slow cooker. Combine remaining ingredients and pour over the ribs. Cover and cook on LOW 6 to 7 hours or until tender. Serve the sauce over the meat. Makes 4 to 6 servings.

Country style pork ribs, a relatively inexpensive cut of meat, are very flavorful and extremely tender when slow cooked. Shred the meat, moisten with some of the sauce and serve on hamburger buns along with cole slaw and baked beans.

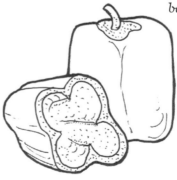

Country Pork Ribs

If you find the pork ribs on sale, this makes for an economical family meal.

2½   pounds boneless country pork ribs
1/3 cup packed light brown sugar
1/3 cup ketchup
1   tablespoon prepared mustard
1   can (15-ounces) sliced peaches, with juice

Place pork ribs in a slow cooker. Combine brown sugar, ketchup, mustard and the juice from the peaches. (Save the peaches to serve as a fruit with your dinner.) Pour sauce over ribs. Cover and cook on LOW 6 to 7 hours or until pork is tender.

Pork Chops & Baked Bean Casserole

Note: You don't have to use the most expensive pork chops for this recipe. The beans and sauce will actually disguise them and they will be wonderfully tender and moist.

4   pork chops, about ¾ inch thick
1   can (28-ounces) brick oven baked beans
½   cup finely chopped onion
½   cup packed light brown sugar
½   cup ketchup
2   teaspoons prepared mustard

Trim fat from pork chops and pat dry. Place in a sprayed slow cooker. Combine remaining ingredients and pour over top. Cover and cook on LOW 5 to 6 hours or until meat is tender. There will be a lot of juice in the pot. To serve remove pork chops and then spoon some of the beans over the top. Makes 4 servings.

Pork Chops with Onion Gravy

4   to 6 large boneless pork chops, 1-1½ inches thick
1   large onion, sliced
1   can (10¾-ounces) condensed Cream of
    Celery soup
    Salt and pepper, if desired

Trim pork chops and pat dry. Place in a sprayed slow cooker. Cover with onion slices. Combine soup with ¼ cup water. Pour over onions. Cover and cook on LOW 5 to 6 hours or until meat is tender. Season with salt and pepper to taste. Makes 4 to 6 servings.

Note: If desired, thicken sauce with 2 tablespoons flour mixed with 4 tablespoons water.

Pork & Sauerkraut

1   3 pound boneless pork loin
    Salt and Pepper
2   jars (32-ounces each) sauerkraut, drained
1   tablespoon caraway seeds
3   cups (12-ounces) Swiss cheese, shredded

Note: If you have a small family, you may want to use only half the sauerkraut, caraway seeds and cheese.

Trim pork of fat and silver skin. Sprinkle with salt and pepper. Place in slow cooker and add ½ cup water. Cover and cook on LOW 4 hours. Remove meat from pot and discard the liquid.

Combine sauerkraut, caraway seeds and cheese. Remove about 2 cups and spoon remaining into pot. Add meat and spoon remaining sauerkraut over top. Cover and continue to cook 1 to 2 hours or until meat is cooked to 140°; it should be tender (it will continue to go up a few degrees after removing from the heat). Makes about 6 servings.

Probably the single most commom mistake in cooking fish and seafood is cooking it too long. In most cases, it takes only minutes in an oven or on a grill and not much longer in a slow cooker. The advantage of a slow cooker is that it eliminates last minute watching at a time when you may have a dozen other things to do. Fish that is a thicker cut and somewhat firm works best in a slow cooker.

Halibut with Roasted Peppers

If you need the answer to a quick fish dish, this is the one. Not only is it easy and very tasty, but it looks great too. No one would ever guess you cooked it in a slow cooker.

1   to 1¼ pounds halibut fillets or steaks
½   cup roasted bell peppers, drained
2   tablespoons light olive oil
3   to 4 dashes hot pepper sauce
2   tablespoons chopped fresh basil
¹/₃   cup freshly grated Parmesan cheese

Cut halibut into serving size pieces, if desired. Place in a sprayed slow cooker.

Place roasted peppers, olive oil and hot sauce in a blender and blend until almost smooth-it's nice to have a few small pieces of pepper. Spoon over fish.

Combine basil and Parmesan and sprinkle over the fish. You may or may not use all the mixture. Cover and cook on LOW 1½ to 2 hours or until halibut is cooked through. Makes 4 servings.

Fillet of Sole

4   to 6 sole fillets, about 1 to 1½ pounds
2   tablespoons butter
1   large onion, sliced
8   ounces fresh mushrooms, sliced
1   cup (4-ounces) Gruyére or Swiss cheese, shredded

Rinse fillets and pat dry. Cook onion in butter until slightly softened. Add mushrooms and cook until soft.

Place half the mixture in a sprayed slow cooker. Sprinkle with half the cheese. Depending on thickness of sole, fold in half or thirds and place over cheese. Add remaining vegetables and cheese. Cover and cook on LOW 2 to 2½ hours or until fish is cooked through. Makes 4 to 6 servings.

Fish in a slow cooker is very moist and flavorful, but you do have to watch carefully to prevent over-cooking.

Hint: Always check for bones before preparing any fish. Rub your hand over both sides of the fish and then remove with needle nose pliers or tweezers.

Salmon Fillets with Pesto

4   (about 6-ounces each) salmon fillets
¼   cup pesto

Place salmon in sprayed slow cooker and brush with pesto. Cover and cook on LOW 1½ to 2 hours or until cooked through. Makes 4 servings.

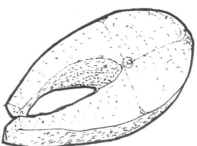

Salmon in a Pot

Fish is faster to do in an oven or on the grill, but if you know you are going to be pressed for time at the last minute, go ahead and start the salmon in your slow cooker and have it cooking while you are busy doing other things.

1½ to 2 pound salmon fillet
¼ cup white wine
2 tablespoons butter, melted
2 tablespoons fresh lemon juice
1 teaspoon soy sauce

Check for bones before placing the salmon in a slow cooker. Combine remaining ingredients and pour over fish. Cover and cook on LOW 1½ to 2 hours. It should be fine the first hour of cooking time, but after that you should watch closely so as not to overcook. Makes 6 to 8 servings.

Tip: Use any leftover salmon for pasta, salads or even on a sandwich. If you don't care for the wine, omit it and add 1 minced garlic clove and 2 tablespoons finely chopped fresh basil or 1 teaspoon dried basil.

Remember:

1 Hour on HIGH=2 Hours on LOW

Florentine Salmon

2 tablespoons butter
¾ cup sliced small fresh mushrooms
1/3 cup sliced green onions
½ bunch fresh spinach
4 (about 6-ounces each) salmon fillets
1/3 cup dry white wine

Quickly sauté mushrooms and onions in butter, in a large skillet. Add spinach and toss to mix. Cook mixture until spinach is just slightly wilted.

Cut a long slit in top of each fillet and spread slightly. Fill pocket with spinach mixture. Place in a sprayed slow cooker and add the wine. Cover and cook on LOW 1½ to 2 hours or until salmon tests done. Makes 4 servings.

Serve with garlic mashed potatoes, sautéed yellow squash and a Caesar salad and you have an easy and delicious company meal.

Orange Roughy

4 (4-ounces each) Orange Roughy fillets
3 tablespoons fresh lemon juice
1 medium garlic clove, finely chopped
½ teaspoon dried dill weed
Salt and pepper to taste

Place fillets, in one layer, in a sprayed slow cooker. Combine lemon juice, garlic and dill weed and brush over fish. Lightly sprinkle with salt and pepper. Cover and cook on LOW 1 hour or until cooked through. Makes 4 servings.

Note: If using fresh dill weed, sprinkle over fish during last half hour of cooking time.

Orange Roughy is a very mild white fish similar to cod.

Tuna Noodle Casserole

We all need a good tuna casserole. This one is easy to assemble and kind to the budget. If desired, sprinkle with Cheddar cheese last ½ hour of cooking time.

4 cups uncooked egg noodles

1 can (10¾-ounces) condensed Cream of Mushroom soup

1/3 cup finely chopped onion, partially cooked

2 cans (6-ounces each) tuna, drained

1 cup frozen peas, thawed

Cook pasta as directed on package; drain.

Meanwhile, combine soup with ¼ cup water in a sprayed slow cooker. Add the pasta along with remaining ingredients. Cover and cook on HIGH 1½ to 2 hours to heat through. Makes 4 to 6 servings.

Menu

*Halibut with Roasted Peppers
Buttered Angel Hair Pasta
Broccoli
*Fantastic Egg Bread
*Lemon Cups

Poultry

Safety Points to Remember

One of the most important things we have to remember in slow cooking is food safety. Earlier I told you how you can check your slow cooker to see how hot it cooks. A temperature of 185° is ideal. Anything below that may not heat the food high enough, or fast enough, to avoid potential food safety problems. A temperature much higher than that, in an 8 hour period, could result in food being overcooked.

According to the United States Department of Agriculture, foods should always be thawed, not frozen. They also suggest not cooking whole chickens or roasts. Even though today's slow cookers cook so much faster than years past, I leave that decision up to you. Always keep perishable foods refrigerated until ready to place in the slow cooker.

When first using your slow cooker, always follow the companies suggestions and guidelines.

Poultry

Poultry is delicious when cooked in a slow cooker and the number of ways it can be prepared are limitless.

Today's slow cookers cook so much faster than they did 10 years ago, and chicken is leaner and often also smaller in size. I don't suggest using the cleaned and ready to cook frozen chicken breasts, only because they are too thin for long slow cooking.

Wash chicken and pat dry before adding to a slow cooker. In most cases, when using chicken pieces, you will want to remove the skin. If you like chicken more firm and dry, use only a very small amount of liquid or eliminate liquid altogether. Chicken with bone-in will usually be more moist and less likely to overcook. Experiment and see which pieces you like best.

Honey Mustard Chicken

In a hurry? This can be prepared in a matter of minutes, leaving you free to do something else.

8	chicken thighs, skinned
¼	cup packed brown sugar
½	cup honey
¼	cup Dijon mustard
2	tablespoons fresh lime or lemon juice

Place chicken in a sprayed slow cooker. Combine remaining ingredients and pour over top. Cover and cook on LOW 6 to 7 hours or until chicken is tender and cooked through. Makes 4 servings.

Note: This recipe creates quite a bit of liquid which also tends to make the chicken cook faster. Watch carefully and check early, if possible. If you want to thicken the sauce, remove chicken and keep warm. Combine 2 tablespoons cornstarch with 2 tablespoons water. Stir into liquid, cover and cook on HIGH 20 to 30 minutes or until thickened.

MENU

*Honey Mustard Chicken
Mashed Potatoes
Green Peas
*Garlic Cheese Bread
*Brownie Sundaes

Chicken with Orange Sauce

8 chicken legs or thighs
1 can (6-ounces) frozen orange juice concentrate, thawed
2 tablespoons sugar
¼ teaspoon salt
2 tablespoons quick-cooking tapioca
¼ cup very finely chopped onion

Place chicken in sprayed slow cooker, in one layer if possible. Combine orange juice, sugar, salt and tapioca. Pour over chicken. Sprinkle onion over top. Cover and cook on LOW 7 to 8 hours or until chicken is tender and cooked through. Makes 4 servings.

I think chicken legs are made for the slow cooker. They can be cooked longer than chicken breasts without drying out, and they turn out moist and delicious.

Cranberry & Apple Chicken

4 to 6 chicken breast halves, skinned and boned
1 can (16-ounces) whole-berry cranberry sauce
1 Golden Delicious apple, chopped
1 teaspoon curry powder
⅓ cup chopped pecans or walnuts
⅓ cup Angel Flake coconut

Place chicken in slow cooker. Combine cranberry sauce, apple and curry; pour over chicken. Cover and cook on LOW 3½ to 4 hours or until chicken is tender and cooked through. Stir in the nuts. Pass coconut at the table. Makes 4 to 6 servings.

Don't omit the coconut. It is that extra touch that really makes this dish.

Curried Chicken Legs

Note: If desired, you can use six chicken legs instead of the eight, but keep in mind leftovers are great too.

8   chicken legs
¾   cup finely chopped onion
½   teaspoon curry powder
1   tablespoon butter, melted
¼   cup orange marmalade

Place chicken in one layer in a slow cooker. Sprinkle onion over top. Combine remaining ingredients and spoon over chicken. Cover and cook on Low 7 to 8 hours or until chicken is tender and cooked through. Makes 4 servings.

Chicken Drumsticks Paprika

8   chicken legs
1   medium onion, sliced
2   teaspoons olive oil
1   teaspoon salt
½   teaspoon pepper
2   teaspoons paprika

Place onion slices in a sprayed slow cooker. Arrange chicken over top, in one layer as much as possible. Combine remaining ingredients with 1 teaspoon water and brush over chicken. Cover and cook on LOW 7 to 8 hours or until chicken is tender and cooked through. Makes 4 servings.

Barbecue Chicken Legs

8   chicken legs, skin removed
½   cup packed light brown sugar
½   cup ketchup
1   tablespoon Worcestershire sauce
1½   teaspoons prepared mustard
2   tablespoons lemon juice

Place chicken in one layer, if possible, in a sprayed slow cooker. Combine remaining ingredients. Remove about $1/3$ cup of the sauce and brush over the chicken. Save remaining sauce to serve with the chicken. Cover and cook on LOW 6 to 7 hours or until chicken is tender and cooked through. Makes 4 servings.

Chicken legs and thighs are very tasty and economical. Purchase in bulk packages, divide and freeze for later use.

Quick Chicken Legs

6   to 8 chicken legs
  Seasoning salt

Place chicken in a sprayed slow cooker, as many in one layer as possible. Sprinkle with seasoning salt. Cover and cook on LOW 7 to 8 hours or until tender and cooked through. Makes 3 to 4 servings.

Note: Do not add any liquid to the slow cooker.

My grandchildren love this recipe. Some of them are now old enough to make it themselves.

Golden Chicken & Mushrooms

A nice family dish. Add a green vegetable, a raw vegetable tray and rolls or cornbread.

4   to 6 chicken breast halves, skinned and boned
1   large onion, thinly sliced
4   to 5 medium potatoes, cut into 1-inch chunks
1   can (10¾-ounces) condensed Golden Mushroom soup

Add onion to a sprayed slow cooker. Top with potatoes and then the chicken. Stir soup and spoon over the chicken. Cover and cook on LOW 7 to 8 hours or until chicken and potatoes are tender. Makes 4 to 6 servings.

Southwestern Chicken Dish

A very good pantry recipe. Just add the chicken and this recipe can be assembled in minutes. Very colorful too.

4   chicken breast halves, skinned and boned
1   tablespoon chili powder
1   can (14.5-ounces) chunky tomatoes, pasta style
1   can (15-ounces) kidney beans, rinsed and drained
1   can (11-ounces) Mexicorn, drained

Place chicken in slow cooker. Combine remaining ingredients and spoon over chicken. Cover and cook on LOW 3½ to 4 hours or until chicken is tender and cooked through. Makes 4 servings.

Fried Chicken

8   chicken legs or other parts
½   cup flour
1   teaspoon salt
½   teaspoon pepper
1   teaspoon paprika
Vegetable Oil

Combine flour, salt, pepper and paprika in a small shallow dish. Coat chicken pieces with the flour mixture.

In a large skillet, heat ¼-inch oil over medium-high heat. Add chicken and quickly brown all sides. Drain on paper towels. Place in slow cooker, keeping as much skin exposed as possible. Cover and cook on LOW 7 to 8 hours or until chicken is tender and cooked through; do not add liquid. Makes 4 servings.

Cream Gravy

4   tablespoons fat from browning chicken
4   tablespoons flour
2   cups milk
Salt and pepper to taste

Place fat in a saucepan and heat until hot. Add flour and stir with a whisk until blended. Cook until just lightly browned, stirring constantly. Add milk and whisk until smooth. Cook, stirring frequently, until gravy is thickened, about 4 to 5 minutes. Add salt and pepper to taste. If gravy is too thick, stir in a little additional milk. If too thin add a little flour mixed with a small amount of water. Makes 2 cups.

Until I tried it, I wasn't sure this was actually a convenient way to cook fried chicken. Since the chicken has to be browned, why not go ahead and cook the chicken all the way. But, browning the chicken doesn't take very long and then I could continue cooking the chicken unattended. I added the chicken to the slow cooker, left for the day and the chicken was cooked to perfection when I got home. If you want cream gravy with your dinner, save 4 tablespoons of the oil from browning the chicken, then follow the recipe for Cream Gravy.

Sweet & Sour Pineapple Chicken

A colorful chicken-pineapple dish. Serve over rice, along with broccoli and hot rolls.

4 to 6 chicken breast halves, skinned and boned
¼ cup packed light brown sugar
1 tablespoon light soy sauce
1 can (16-ounces) pineapple chunks with juice
½ small green pepper, cut into narrow strips
½ red pepper, cut into narrow strips

Place chicken in slow cooker. In a small bowl, combine brown sugar, soy sauce and the pineapple juice. Pour mixture over the chicken; add pineapple chunks. Cover and cook on LOW 3 to 3½ hours.

Add pepper strips. Cover and cook on HIGH 20 to 30 minutes or until peppers are just crisp tender.

Sherried Chicken

10 chicken legs
1 medium onion, sliced
4 ounces fresh mushrooms, sliced
½ cup dry sherry
1 teaspoon Italian seasoning

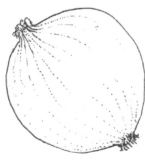

Place onion and mushrooms in slow cooker. Top with chicken; add sherry and sprinkle with seasoning. Cover and cook on LOW 7 to 8 hours or until chicken is cooked through and tender. Makes 4 servings.

Company Cornish Hens

2   Cornish Hens, halved
1   can (15-ounces) dark sweet cherries in syrup
2   tablespoons dry Sherry
2   tablespoons cornstarch
½   cup chili sauce
1   medium garlic clove, minced

Rinse Cornish hens and pat dry. Place in a sprayed slow cooker, skin-side up and in one layer, if possible.

Drain syrup from the cherries and combine the syrup with the Sherry and cornstarch, mixing until smooth. Add chili sauce and garlic and add to slow cooker. Spoon cherries over top. Cover and cook on LOW 4 to 4½ hours or until tender and cooked through. Makes 2 to 4 servings.

Spoon the wonderful sauce over Cornish hens and serve with rice pilaf, a green bean casserole, and hot buttered rolls.

Tip: To halve the Cornish hens, first thaw and then cut from one end of the back to the other. This is very easy to do with a pair of kitchen scissors. Then cut or trim off the back bones.

Broccoli-Cheese Chicken

The chicken is extremely moist and tender, with a very mild broccoli-cheese flavor. For a more pro- nounced broc- coli taste, serve with steamed fresh broccoli spears.

4   chicken breast halves, skinned and boned
¼   cup finely chopped onion
½   cup milk
1   can (10¾-ounces) condensed Broccoli
     Cheese soup

Place chicken in a sprayed slow cooker. Sprinkle with onion.Combine milk and soup and mix well; pour over the chicken. Cover and cook on LOW 3½ to 4 hours or until chicken is tender and cooked through. Makes 4 servings.

Italian Chicken

A nice, kind to the budget, family type dish. It may not be fancy, but the chicken is unbe- lievably tender.

8   chicken legs, skin removed
1   teaspoon Italian seasoning
1   teaspoon packed light brown sugar
1   can (8-ounces) tomato sauce
½   of a small onion

Place chicken in a slow cooker. Combine Italian season- ing, sugar and tomato sauce and spoon over chicken.

Cut onion into thirds, separate sections and scatter over chicken. Cover and cook on LOW 6 to 7 hours or until chicken is tender and cooked through. Spoon sauce over chicken when serving. Makes 4 servings.

Garlic Chicken & Potatoes

1	chicken, cut up
4	medium potatoes, peeled and quartered
8	large garlic cloves
¼	cup butter, melted
¼	cup honey
½	teaspoon lemon pepper

Place potatoes in slow cooker. Arrange chicken over top. Add garlic. Drizzle butter and honey over chicken. Sprinkle with lemon pepper. Cover and cook on LOW 5 to 6 hours or until chicken is tender and potatoes are cooked through. Makes 4 servings.

The aroma of this dish will entice everyone into the kitchen.

Tip: Remove the thin paper-like skin from garlic cloves, but do not peel.

Busy Day Chicken Legs

8	chicken legs
	Paprika
	Garlic salt
	Lemon Pepper

Place chicken in one layer in a sprayed slow cooker. Sprinkle with paprika, garlic salt and lemon pepper; do not add any liquid. Cover and cook on LOW 6 to 7 hours or until chicken is cooked through. The chicken should be nicely browned. Makes 4 servings.

Follow the recipe exactly, remove chicken and place on a serving plate, and unless you tell them, your family or guests will never know you used a slow cooker.

Honey-Ginger Chicken

This is one of those recipes that starts out looking rather pale, but eventually takes on a beautiful rich brown color. Serve with garlic mashed potatoes, peas and hot corn bread.

6   to 8 chicken thighs
1/3 cup butter, melted
1/3 cup honey
2   tablespoons lemon juice
1   teaspoon ground ginger

Place chicken in a sprayed slow cooker. Combine remaining ingredients and pour over chicken. Cover and cook on LOW 5 to 5½ hours or until chicken is tender and cooked through. If you are home, spoon liquid over chicken 2 or 3 times during last half of cooking time. Serve chicken with a small amount of sauce spooned over the top. Makes 3 to 4 servings.

Creamed Chicken with Almonds

One of my comfort foods. Nice and creamy and delicious served over rice or mashed potatoes.

4   chicken breast halves, skinned and boned
1   package (3-ounces) cream cheese, softened
1   can (10¾-ounces) condensed Cream of Celery soup
2   tablespoons slivered almonds

Place chicken in a sprayed slow cooker. In a small bowl, beat cream cheese with mixer until fluffy. Add soup and beat until well mixed. Pour over chicken. Sprinkle with almonds. Cover and cook on LOW 2½ to 3½ hours or until chicken is tender and cooked through. Stir sauce before serving. Makes 4 servings.

Roasting Chicken & Potatoes

1	4 to 4½ pound chicken
2	medium onions, sliced
4	small potatoes, peeled and halved
¾	teaspoon dried rosemary or Italian seasoning
2	medium garlic cloves, minced

Place onion over bottom of a slow cooker. Place chicken on top. Sprinkle with seasoning and garlic. Arrange potatoes around outside of chicken placing next to the sides of the slow cooker. Add ½ cup water. (Push the potatoes down into the pot as more liquid accumulates.) Cover and cook on Low 8 to 9 hours or until chicken is tender and a thermometer inserted in the thigh reads 170°. Remove from pot and let stand 10 to 15 minutes before serving. Makes 6 servings.

If cooked to just the right temperature, you will not be able to tell the chicken was cooked in a slow cooker. It will be moist and slice beautifully.

Mushroom Garlic Chicken

8	chicken legs or thighs
1¼	cups chopped onion
1	can (10¾-ounces) condensed Cream of Mushroom soup with Roasted Garlic

Add onion to slow cooker. Arrange chicken over top. Spoon soup over chicken to coat. Cover and cook on LOW 6 to 7 hours or until chicken is tender and cooked through. Makes 4 servings.

Southwestern Style Chicken

A nice southwestern flavor packed into just four ingredients. Takes less than 10 minutes to assemble.

4   to 6 chicken breast halves, skinned and boned
1   jar (16-ounces) chunky salsa, divided
2   cups frozen corn, thawed
1   can (15-ounces) black beans, drained

Combine half of the salsa, and all the corn and black beans in a slow cooker. Add chicken; top with remaining salsa. Cover and cook on LOW 4 to 5 hours or until chicken is tender and cooked through. Makes 4 to 6 servings.

Note

Some chicken breasts are quite thin and will take less time to cook than the thicker ones. Four chicken breasts may also take less time to cook than if you use six chicken breasts. If possible, check for doneness during last hour of cooking time. Overcooked chicken may appear tender, but will be quite dry.

Rosemary Chicken

1   3 to 4 pound chicken
4   medium potatoes
1   teaspoon olive oil
1   teaspoon dried rosemary

Cut potatoes into 1½-inch chunks, and place in slow cooker. Add ½ cup water. Place chicken over potatoes. Brush chicken with oil and sprinkle with rosemary. Cover and cook on LOW 7 to 8 hours or until chicken is tender and cooked through. Watch carefully after 6 hours. Makes 4 servings.

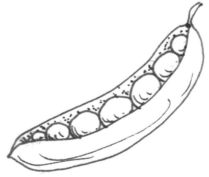

Chicken & Green Bean Casserole

2 cups cubed cooked chicken
1 can (14.5-ounces) French style green beans
1 can (5-ounces) sliced water chestnuts, drained
1 package (6-ounces) Long-Grain and Wild Rice mix with seasoning packet
1 cup mayonnaise
1 can (10¾-ounces) condensed Cream of Mushroom soup

Place chicken, drained green beans, water chestnuts and rice with seasoning packet, in a sprayed slow cooker. Combine mayonnaise and soup and mix to blend. Gradually stir in 2¼ cups water. Add to slow cooker and stir ingredients to mix. Cover and cook on LOW 5 to 6 hours or until rice is tender. Makes 6 to 8 servings.

A great way to use up leftover chicken or turkey and also sneak in one of your green vegetables for the day.

Cranberry Chicken

4 chicken breast halves, skinned and boned
½ cup finely chopped onion
1 cup barbecue sauce
1 can (16-ounces) whole berry cranberry sauce

Place chicken in a sprayed slow cooker. Combine remaining ingredients and pour over the chicken. Cover and cook on LOW 3½ to 4 hours or until chicken is tender and cooked through. Makes 4 servings.

The type of barbecue sauce used will ultimately decide the flavor of the dish. I find a sweet BBQ sauce is more compatible with the sweetness of the cranberries.

Roast Chicken

On those days when you are going to be gone all day and need something to cook for 8 to 10 hours, choose a chicken at least 4 to 5 pounds.

1   4 to 5 pound chicken
1   teaspoon dried Italian herbs
¼   teaspoon pepper
2   garlic cloves, minced
1   large onion, sliced
4   medium potatoes, peeled and halved

With your fingers, carefully loosen the skin covering the breast and leg area. Combine herbs, pepper and minced garlic. Carefully spread mixture under the skin, spreading evenly.

Separate onion slices into rings and place in a large (about 5 quart) slow cooker. Place chicken over onions. Place potato slices around the chicken next to the pot. It may be a little crowded, but press potatoes down as far as they will go. Cover and bake on LOW 8 to 10 hours or until temperature reaches 170°. Makes 6 servings.

A frequently asked question is whether or not we should wash chicken before cooking. Some will say no, but I prefer to wash the chicken first. I then remove the excess fat, etc...

With so many problems in the poultry and meat industry, I don't think it hurts to take that extra precautionary step to prevent a possible future illness. Frozen, ready to cook chicken breasts, nuggets, etc. are an exception. They have been cleaned and trimmed and are ready to cook.

Roast Chicken with Pesto

1   4 to 4½ pound chicken
½   cup pesto (approximate)
     Salt and pepper

Carefully loosen the skin from the breast, leg and thigh areas, being careful not to tear the skin. Spoon some of the pesto into each of these areas and press on the skin to more evenly distribute the sauce. Tie the leg ends together, if desired, using string or dental floss.

Place chicken in a sprayed slow cooker and sprinkle with salt and pepper. Cover and bake on LOW 7 to 8 hours or until chicken is tender and cooked through. Remove chicken, cover with foil, and let stand 10 to 15 minutes before slicing. Makes 6 servings.

It is easy to overcook chicken in a slow cooker. If cooked too long, the chicken will completely fall apart when trying to remove from the pot. The chicken will be tender, but often has an almost burnt taste. By cooking to a thigh temperature of 170°, the chicken can be removed intact and will be fork-tender and moist.

Chicken & Apple Dish

4   chicken breast halves, skinned and boned
2   apples, peeled, cut into ¼" slices
¼   cup apple cider
¼   cup dried cherries or cranberries
8   fresh sage leaves
     Pepper

Rinse chicken and pat dry. Place apples in a slow cooker; arrange chicken over top. Add cider and cherries. Place 2 sage leaves on each chicken breast. Sprinkle with pepper. Cover and bake on LOW 4 to 5 hours or until chicken is cooked through. Makes 4 servings.

Chicken & Rice Casserole

This quick and easy recipe can be assembled in 10 minutes, or even less if the chicken has already been washed and trimmed.

4 chicken breast halves, skinned and boned
1 cup uncooked long-grain rice
1 package onion soup mix
1 can (10¾-ounces) condensed Cream of Chicken soup

Combine rice and onion soup mix in a sprayed slow cooker. Top with chicken pieces.

Combine the chicken soup with 1½ soup cans water, mixing until smooth. Pour over chicken. Cover and cook on LOW 4½ to 5 hours, stirring mixture about midway through cooking time to more evenly distribute the rice. Cook until liquid is absorbed and rice is tender. Makes 4 servings.

Curried Chicken

To Serve: Curries cry out for an accompaniment of something sweet such as a chutney, coconut, peanuts, raisins, orange pieces, etc. Serve over rice with accompaniments on the side.

4 chicken breast halves, skinned and boned
¼ cup butter, melted
¼ cup honey
2 tablespoons prepared mustard
½ teaspoon curry powder
½ teaspoon salt

Place chicken in slow cooker. Combine remaining ingredients and pour over chicken. Cover and cook on LOW 3 to 4 hours or until chicken is cooked through. Makes 4 servings.

Chicken Italian with Rice

4   large chicken breast halves, skinned and boned
1   cup uncooked long-grain rice
1   package (.65-ounce) Italian dressing mix
1   can (10¾-ounces) condensed Cream of
    Chicken soup

Place rice in slow cooker. Combine dressing mix and soup. Gradually stir in 1¾ cup water; pour over rice. Place chicken over top. Cover and cook on LOW 3 to 4 hours or until rice is tender and chicken is cooked through. Makes 4 servings.

I prepare this recipe so often in the oven that I decided to try it in the slow cooker. This is convenient on days when I am out of the house for just a few hours.

Chicken with Chutney & Pineapple

4   large chicken breast halves, skinned and boned
½   cup Major Grey's chutney
¼   cup prepared mustard
1   can (8-ounces) pineapple tidbits, drained
1/3 cup sliced almonds

Place chicken in a sprayed slow cooker. Combine chutney and mustard in a small bowl. Add pineapple and almonds. Spread mixture over chicken. Cover and cook on HIGH 3 to 3½ hours. Makes 4 servings.

Serve chicken and sauce over a bed of rice. Add a green vegetable, hot rolls and a yummy dessert.

Tip

This dish accumulates more liquid when cooked on LOW, and has more flavor and somewhat less liquid when cooked on HIGH.

Company Chicken & Rice

4   chicken breast halves
1   package (6-ounces) Long-grain and Wild Rice mix
    with seasoning packet
¼   cup chopped pecans
1   jar (2-ounces) pimientos, drained and chopped
2   cups orange juice

Clean chicken and pat dry. Combine remaining ingredients in a sprayed slow cooker. Arrange chicken over top. Cover and cook on LOW 5 to 6 hours or just until the rice is tender and the chicken is cooked through. Makes 4 servings.

Note: I used bone-in chicken breasts that were quite large, but they cooked in the same amount of time as the rice. You could also use a cut up chicken or all chicken legs, if desired.

Cooked Chicken

Chicken breasts or parts, with skin
Salt and pepper
2   stalks celery, coarsely chopped
½   cup chopped onion
2   carrots, coarsely chopped

Place chicken in slow cooker. Sprinkle with salt and pepper. Add remaining ingredients. Add 2 to 4 cups of water to cover the chicken. Cover and cook on LOW 4 to 5 hours or until cooked through.

When you need a lot of cooked chicken for casseroles, salad and soups, it is so easy to just cook it in your slow cooker.

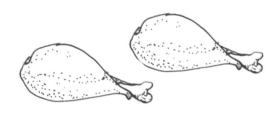

Saucy Chicken Legs

8	chicken legs
1	large garlic clove, minced
1/3	cup light soy sauce
1½	tablespoons ketchup

The soy sauce adds a lot of color to the finished dish.

Place chicken legs in one layer in a slow cooker.

Combine remaining ingredients and pour over chicken. Cover and cook on LOW 7 to 8 hours or until chicken is tender and cooked through. If possible, baste chicken with sauce twice during the last two hours of cooking time. Makes 4 servings.

Italian Garlic Chicken

4	chicken breast halves, skinned and boned
1	package (0.65-ounces) Cheese Garlic dressing mix
4	ounces cream cheese, softened
1	can (10¾-ounces) condensed Cream of Chicken soup
	Fresh or dried parsley

Note: By partially cooking the chicken, then removing the liquid before adding the soup mixture, it will make a nice thick sauce rather than one that is too thin.

Place chicken in a slow cooker. Combine the dressing mix with 1/3 cup water and pour over the chicken. Cover and cook on LOW 3 hours. Remove liquid from the pot.

Place cream cheese in a medium mixing bowl. Gradually beat in the soup, mixing until smooth. Spoon over chicken and sprinkle with parsley. Cover and cook on LOW 1 hour or until chicken is tender and cooked through. Makes 4 servings.

Variation: Substitute Italian dressing mix for the Cheese Garlic dressing. Sprinkle with sliced almonds.

Creamed Chicken with Tarragon

A subtle tarragon flavored sauce that is very good served over rice.

4	to 6 chicken breast halves, skinned and boned
1/3	cup chopped onion
1/2	teaspoon dried leaf tarragon
2	tablespoons butter, melted
1/3	cup dry sherry
1	can (10¾-ounces) condensed Cream of Chicken soup

Place chicken in slow cooker. Combine remaining ingredients and pour over the chicken. Cover and cook on LOW 3½ to 4 hours or until chicken is tender and cooked through. Makes 4 to 6 servings.

Note: *A lot of older slow cooker recipes will tell you to cook boneless chicken breasts on LOW for 6 to 8 hours. Today's chicken breasts are leaner and often very thin compared to what we used to buy years ago. If the chicken pieces are quite thick and you have several pieces in the pot, it may take a little longer, otherwise watch cooking time closely to prevent overcooking.*

Sweet & Hot Chicken Thighs

8	chicken thighs, skinned
1/2	cup apricot preserves
1/4	cup ketchup
2	tablespoons soy sauce
1/2	teaspoon hot pepper sauce

Place chicken, rounded side up, in one layer, in a slow cooker. Combine remaining ingredients and spoon over chicken. Cover and cook on LOW 4 to 5 hours or until chicken is tender and cooked through. Makes 4 servings.

Everyday Chicken

6   chicken legs, skin removed
¼   cup ketchup
¼   cup regular cola flavored soft drink, not diet
     Fresh or dried parsley

Place chicken in a slow cooker. Combine ketchup and cola and pour over top. Sprinkle with parsley. Cover and cook on LOW 6 to 7 hours or until cooked through. Makes 3 servings.

Note: *The next time you have a cola save ¼ cup for this recipe. It is okay if it is flat. The pop adds sweetness to the recipe, and if you were baking the recipe in the oven, it would make a nice glaze.*

Easy Chicken & Wild Rice Dish

4   large chicken breast halves, skinned and boned
1½   cups finely chopped onion
1   can (10¾-ounces) condensed Broccoli Cheese soup
2   packages (6-ounces each) Long-grain and Wild Rice mix with seasoning packet
8   ounces process cheese spread, cubed

Cut chicken lengthwise into ¼ inch slices. Cut each slice crosswise into narrow strips. Place in a sprayed slow cooker along with 2¾ cups water and remaining ingredients. Cover and cook on LOW 4 to 5 hours or until liquid is absorbed and rice is tender. Makes 8 servings.

Note: *Start watching carefully after 4 hours cooking time, rice can vary somewhat, especially in a slow cooker.*

Mushroom Chicken with Sour Cream

On those busy days, this just takes minutes to put together. Serve over rice or noodles or serve with mashed potatoes. For added color, sprinkle with toasted almonds, parsley, or cooked bacon pieces.

6   chicken breast halves, skinned and boned
1   can (14-ounces) condensed Cream of Mushroom soup
1   cup sour cream

Place chicken in a sprayed slow cooker. Combine soup and sour cream and spoon over chicken. Cover and cook on LOW 3½ to 4 hours or until chicken is cooked through. The soup mixture may separate a little around the edge, but it can be stirred to make a smooth creamy sauce. Makes 6 servings.

Tomato & Tarragon Chicken

If you aren't a tarragon fan, you can substitute basil, oregano or mixed herbs.

8   chicken thighs or legs
¹/₃   cup chopped onion
4   plum tomatoes, chopped
1   large garlic clove, minced
½   teaspoon dried tarragon
½   teaspoon salt

Place chicken in a slow cooker. Add remaining ingredients. Cover and cook on LOW 6 hours or until cooked through. Makes 4 servings.

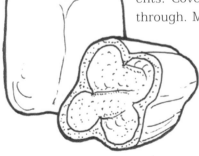

Orange & Basil Chicken

8 chicken legs
1 cup chopped onion
¹/₃ cup frozen orange juice concentrate, thawed
½ teaspoon dried basil, crushed
Salt and pepper

Rinse chicken and pat dry. Spread onion in a sprayed slow cooker. Arrange chicken over top. Pour orange concentrate over the chicken. Sprinkle with basil, salt and pepper. Cover and cook on LOW 4 to 5 hours or until chicken is tender. Makes 4 servings.

A very mild orange-basil flavor. If gravy is desired, combine 2 tablespoons cornstarch with about 2 tablespoons cold water. Stir into liquid. Cover and cook on HIGH 8 to 10 minutes.

Lemon Pepper Chicken

1 3 to 4 pound chicken
1 medium onion
Lemon pepper

Trim chicken. Cut onion into quarters and separate. Place ¼ of the slices in chicken cavity. Scatter remaining in bottom of slow cooker. Place chicken over onions and add ¼ cup water. Sprinkle chicken with lemon pepper. Cover and cook on LOW about 7 to 8 hours or until chicken is tender. Watch carefully after 6 hours. Remove chicken, cover with foil, and let stand 10 to 15 minutes. Makes 4 to 6 servings.

Slow cooked chicken makes an excellent dinner meal, but it's also a convenient way to cook chicken for sandwiches, salads and casseroles.

Apricot Glazed Turkey Breast

Serve with mashed potatoes or a rice casserole, fresh asparagus and coleslaw. Or slice for sandwiches.

1	2½ to 3 pound turkey breast half
½	cup apricot preserves
1	tablespoon prepared mustard
2	teaspoons Worcestershire sauce
½	teaspoon coarsely ground black pepper

Place turkey breast in a sprayed slow cooker. Combine remaining ingredients and spread over top. Cover and cook on LOW 8 to 9 hours or until temperature reaches 160°. Makes 6 servings.

Turkey Legs

Turkey legs take considerably longer to cook than chicken legs. We're looking at about 10 to 12 hours on LOW. If you don't have that much time, consider cooking on HIGH about 5½ to 6 hours. If desired, make gravy with the drippings.

3	turkey legs
	Oil
	Paprika
	Seasoning salt
	Garlic salt
	Mixed herbs

Place turkey legs in a sprayed slow cooker. Brush lightly with oil. Sprinkle with seasonings. Cover and cook on LOW 10 to 12 hours or until tender. Makes 3 to 4 servings.

Slow Cooker Stuffing

1	package (12-ounces) sausage
1	cup chopped onion
6	cups seasoned stuffing bread cubes
1/3	cup dried cranberries
2/3	cup chopped pecans
1	can (14-ounces) chicken broth

In medium skillet, cook sausage and onion until cooked through; do not drain. Meanwhile, place bread cubes, cranberries and pecans in a large mixing bowl. Add sausage. Add chicken broth and toss until well mixed. If dressing seems too dry for you, add a little more broth. Place in a sprayed slow cooker. Cover and cook 2 to 3 hours or until hot. Makes 8 cups

Note: You can also add more broth while the dressing is cooking; just a small amount at a time.

As much as I love to bake stuffing in the turkey, I have to admit, this is a lot easier. If it is your turn to take the stuffing for a turkey dinner, cook it in your slow cooker and plug it in when you get there. It will keep hot until ready to serve.

MENU

*Apricot Glazed Turkey Breast
Scalloped Potatoes
Yellow Squash & Zucchini
*Rustic Apple Pie

Roast Chicken & Rice Stuffing

1   4 to 4½ pound chicken
1   package (6-ounces) Long-grain and Wild Rice mix with seasoning packet
⅓ cup chopped pecans
    Salt and pepper
    Parsley, dried or chopped fresh

Cook rice according to directions on package. Add pecans. Spoon rice into cavity of the chicken, but pack loosely. You will have some rice left over.

If desired, tie legs with string or dental floss. Place in a sprayed slow cooker. Cover and cook on LOW 4½ to 5½ hours or until chicken is tender and cooked through. Juices should run clear and the thigh temperature should be 170°. Remove chicken, cover with foil, and let stand 10 to 15 minutes before slicing. Makes 6 servings.

Keep
It
Hot

Keep-it Hot

Most of us use our slow cooker for long slow cooking and rarely think to use it any other way. In this section I have tried to show you other ways to take advantage of this great "kitchen helper."

Casseroles are usually baked in an oven, but many can be cooked in a slow cooker, thus freeing up your oven for other things. In this section I show you the easiest way I know to make Chicken Fettuccine and keep it hot until ready to serve. This is a must try recipe.

After making some of these dishes, you may want to experiment with some of your favorite recipes. Just remember that pasta and rice can work very well in a slow cooker, but watch carefully to prevent over-cooking.

*K*eep it Hot recipes are recipes that would normally be baked in the oven, but can be cooked in a slow cooker, mainly for convenience. They can be cooked through, or just kept hot, freeing you from any last minute details. It is also ideal for pot luck recipes and buffets. I'm sure you can find many of your own recipes that you will want to use in this way.

Hamburger Hot Dish

5	cups cooked rotini (spiral-shaped) noodles
1½	pounds lean ground beef
¾	cup chopped onion
1	cup sour cream
1	can (10¾-ounces) condensed Cream of Chicken soup
1	can (10¾-ounces) condensed Cream of Mushroom soup

Cook pasta until just cooked through; do not overcook. Drain.

Meanwhile, in a large skillet, brown ground beef and onion; drain. Stir in the sour cream and soups. Add pasta and heat through. Pour mixture into a slow cooker. Cover and keep hot on LOW. Makes 6 to 8 servings.

Don't keep on the LOW setting more than 45 to 60 minutes or the noodles will become quite soft. You can also heat on LOW until the outside of the slow cooker is hot, then turn off and keep covered until ready to serve.

Soft Beef Taco Casserole

Note: Flour tortillas are easier to roll if they are softened. Cover with wax paper or wrap in paper towels and microwave about 1 minute. Time may vary in different microwaves.

1	pound lean ground beef
1	small green pepper, cubed
1	cup chunky salsa
1/3	cup sour cream
8	(8-inch) flour tortillas
1½	cups (6-ounces) Cheddar cheese, shredded

Brown ground beef and green pepper in a medium skillet; drain. Add salsa and stir to mix.

Spread each tortilla with a little sour cream. Spoon about 2 tablespoons of the meat mixture on each tortilla and wrap to secure filling. Place, seam side down, in a sprayed slow cooker. Spoon remaining meat mixture over top. Sprinkle with the cheese making sure all the tortillas are completely covered. Cover and cook on LOW 1½ to 2 hours or until heated through. Makes 4 servings.

Hawaiian Ham & Rice

The brown sugar is just the added flavor this recipe needs.

2	cans (8-ounces each) crushed pineapple with juice
1	cup uncooked long-grain rice
½	cup packed light brown sugar
1	teaspoon Dijon mustard
2	cups cubed ham

In a saucepan, combine 1½ cups water with ½ cup of the pineapple juice. Bring to a boil and add the rice. Reduce heat, cover and cook 20 minutes or until liquid is absorbed. Remove from heat and stir in the pineapple, brown sugar, mustard and then the ham. Spoon into a sprayed slow cooker, cover and cook on LOW until heated and up to 1½ hours. Makes 6 servings.

Sausage Pasta Casserole

8   ounces penne
1   pound sausage
1   cup chopped onion
1   jar (28-ounces) spaghetti sauce with mushrooms
½   cup sliced ripe olives
½   cup (4-ounces) Mozzarella, shredded

Cook pasta following package directions, cooking a minute or two less than you normally would; drain. Meanwhile, brown sausage and onion until cooked through; drain. Place in a sprayed slow cooker along with the pasta, sauce and olives. Cover and cook on LOW 2 to 2½ hours or until very hot. Sprinkle cheese on top, cover and continue to cook 20 to 30 minutes or until cheese has melted. Makes 6 servings.

This is a wonderfully easy dish to double and serve buffet style right from the slow cooker. Add a large tossed green salad with a tasty home-made dressing, toasted French bread and one of your favorite desserts.

Sausage Penne Pasta

1   pound sausage
¾   cup chopped onion
16 ounces Penne pasta
1   jar (28-ounces) spaghetti sauce
2   cups (8-ounces) Monterey Jack cheese, shredded

The pasta may cook faster than the meat, so start the sausage first.

Brown the sausage and onion; drain. Add spaghetti sauce and heat through.

Meanwhile, cook the pasta according to package directions. Drain and return to the pot. Add meat sauce and toss. Pour half the mixture into a sprayed slow cooker. Sprinkle with half the cheese. Add remaining pasta and sprinkle with remaining cheese. Cover and cook on LOW, about 1½ hours. Any longer than that and it may get too brown around the edges. Makes about 10 servings.

Chicken Pasta Casserole

A very good
family type dish
and a great way
to use up any
leftover chicken.

Variation: Use
ham and cream
of chicken soup.

8	ounces rigatoni or penne pasta
2½	cups cooked cubed chicken
2	cups (8-ounces) Swiss cheese, shredded
1	can (10¾-ounces) condensed Cream of Mushroom soup
½	cup milk

Cook pasta according to package directions; rinse until cool and drain. Place in a sprayed slow cooker. Add chicken and cheese. Combine soup and milk until smooth. Add to slow cooker and toss to coat. Cover and bake on LOW 2½ to 3 hours. Makes 6 servings.

Broccoli-Pasta Dish

This is ideal for
an occasional
"no meat"
meal. Add a
salad, toasted
bread and
perhaps your
favorite dessert
or fruit.

8	ounces penne or rotini pasta
4	cups frozen broccoli florettes and stems, do not thaw
¼	cup olive oil
1	small garlic, minced
¼	teaspoon crushed red pepper
½	cup plus 2 tablespoons grated Parmesan cheese

Add the pasta and broccoli to boiling water. Cook the pasta according to package directions; drain. The broccoli may be finished before the pasta. If so, it is easy to remove, because it tends to float to the top and the pasta tends to sink to the bottom.

Add olive oil, garlic, pepper and ½ cup Parmesan cheese to slow cooker. Add pasta and broccoli. Sprinkle with remaining cheese. Cover and cook on LOW at the most 2 hours. Makes about 6 side dish servings or 4 main dish servings.

Spaghetti with Garlic & Chicken

16 ounces spaghetti
4   chicken breast halves, skinned and boned
½   cup olive oil
2   large garlic cloves, minced
¼   cup chopped fresh parsley
½   cup freshly grated Parmesan cheese

There's only one thing to say about this recipe. Delicious!

Cook pasta according to package directions; drain and return to pot. Meanwhile, cut chicken breasts crosswise into ½-inch slices. Toss with 1 tablespoon of the oil. Heat remaining oil in large skillet. Add chicken and sauté over medium-high heat, stirring almost constantly. Just before chicken is done, add garlic and cook, stirring constantly. Remove from heat and stir in parsley. Pour into a sprayed slow cooker. Add pasta and cheese and toss to mix. If mixture seems a little dry, add additional oil or some of the hot pasta water. Cover and keep warm on LOW until ready to serve. Should keep at least an hour. Makes 6 servings.

Hot Dinner Rolls

A slow cooker is ideal for heating rolls. Place in slow cooker, cover and heat on LOW about 1 to 1½ hours or until heated through. The time will depend on how many rolls you are heating.

Baked Fettuccine

A wonderful pasta side dish with a slightly sweet flavor. The light almost custard type mixture tends to settle toward the bottom, so spoon deep when serving.

8   ounces Fettuccine
¼   cup butter
½   cup half and half
2   large eggs, lightly beaten
3   tablespoons freshly grated Parmesan cheese
    Paprika or chopped parsley

Cook pasta according to package directions; drain well and return to pot. Stir in butter until melted. Combine half and half and eggs. Add to pasta along with the Parmesan. Spoon into a sprayed slow cooker; sprinkle lightly with paprika or parsley. Cover and cook on LOW 2 hours or just until heated through. Makes 6 side dish servings.

How long should I cook the pasta?

The pasta should be cooked just before the al denté stage. Do not overcook at this point. Two hours is just about right for the slow cooker cooking time. Anything longer and the pasta may become too soft.

Cheesy Tomato Spaghetti

16 ounces spaghetti
1 tablespoon olive oil
3 large eggs, lightly beaten
1¼ cups freshly grated Parmesan cheese
1 cup (4-ounces) Mozzarella cheese, shredded
1 jar (28-ounces) tomato-basil spaghetti sauce

Cook pasta according to directions on package. Drain and rinse with cold water to cool. Place in a sprayed slow cooker. Toss with olive oil.

Combine eggs and Parmesan cheese. Stir in the Mozzarella. Add to the slow cooker and toss thoroughly with the pasta. Make a shallow bed in the center. Spread the sauce in the bed. Cover and cook on HIGH 1½ to 2 hours or until heated through. Makes about 6 servings.

You could add ground beef or turkey to the spaghetti sauce, but I doubt your family will miss it, especially if you embellish the dinner with maybe home-made brownies and ice cream.

Fettuccine & Ham

12 ounces Fettuccine
¼ cup butter, cubed
1 cup half and half
2 cups frozen peas, thawed
1 cup diced ham
½ cup freshly grated Parmesan cheese

Cook pasta according to directions on package; drain. Add pasta and butter to a sprayed slow cooker and toss until butter is melted; add remaining ingredients. Cover and cook on LOW until heated through, and probably for no more than an hour, or it will tend to get a little dry. If this should happen, stir in additional half and half. Makes 6 servings.

The most time consuming part of this recipe is cooking the pasta. The rest is easy.

Chicken Enchiladas

If you like soft creamy dishes, you will like this quick to assemble recipe that makes its own sauce.

2   cups cubed cooked chicken

3   cups (12-ounces) Monterey Jack cheese with peppers, shredded

1   can (10¾-ounces) condensed Cream of Chicken soup

½   cup milk

6   (8-inch) flour tortillas

Combine chicken and cheese and set aside. Combine milk and soup, beating until smooth and set aside.

Place about ½ cup or more chicken mixture on each tortilla and roll. Place, seam side down, in a sprayed slow cooker. If using an oval shaped pot, they should fit in one layer. In a round pot, you may have to stack them. Pour soup mixture over enchiladas covering completely. Sprinkle remaining chicken mixture over top. Cover and cook on HIGH about 2 hours or until heated through. Makes 4 servings.

Hint

To avoid mishaps and missing ingredients, always read through the entire recipe before preparing a dish. I also like to assemble and measure all of the ingredients before I begin.

Spaghetti Carbonara

12	ounces spaghetti
12	slices bacon, cooked and crumbled
½	cup butter, cubed
3	large eggs, lightly beaten
1	cup freshly grated Parmesan cheese

Cook pasta according to directions on package. Drain, but save about ½ cup of the liquid and set aside. Place pasta in a sprayed slow cooker. Add bacon, butter, eggs and cheese and toss to coat. If mixture seems a little dry, add some of the pasta water. Cover and cook on LOW to finish cooking the eggs and to keep the pasta hot. It should keep for about an hour without drying out. Makes 4 to 6 servings.

By cooking the final stages of the recipe in a slow cooker, you can rest assured the eggs will be cooked through.

Ham & Cheese Mostaccioli

8	ounces Mostaccioli pasta
1	bunch green onions, about 7 or 8
2	teaspoons vegetable oil
3	tablespoons sliced almonds
2	cups small cubed ham
¾	cup freshly grated Parmesan cheese, divided

Cook pasta according to package directions, but cook about 2 minutes less, or until not quite cooked through. Drain off water and rinse until pasta is cool.

Meanwhile, slice onions into ½-inch slices. Heat oil in a small skillet and cook onion until just tender. Place in a sprayed slow cooker along with the almonds and ham. Add the pasta and toss to coat. Add Parmesan cheese and toss well to mix. Cover and cook on HIGH 2 to 2½ hours. Makes 4 servings.

Cheesy Ground Beef & Pepperoni Casserole

Just as pleasing a dish for company as for family. Add a nice large tossed salad with Italian dressing, fresh hot buttered French bread and spumoni ice cream, if you can find it.

1½	pounds lean ground beef
28	ounces chunky spaghetti sauce with mushrooms
12	ounces penne pasta
1	package (3.5-ounces) sliced pepperoni
3	cups (12-ounces) Cheddar cheese, shredded
3	cups (12-ounces) Mozzarella cheese, shredded

Brown the ground beef; drain. Add spaghetti sauce and heat through. Meanwhile, cook pasta according to package directions; drain.

In a sprayed slow cooker, layer one third meat, pasta, pepperoni, Cheddar and Mozzarella cheese. Repeat each layer two more times ending with the Mozzarella cheese. Cover and cook on HIGH 1½ to 2 hours or until nice and hot. Makes 8 servings.

Pasta & Cheese Casserole

Spaghetti is always a hit, whether for family, buffet or a potluck.

12	ounces spaghetti
1	pound lean ground beef
1	cup chopped onion
1	jar (28-ounces) chunky spaghetti sauce
2	cups (8-ounces) Mozzarella cheese, shredded
2	cups (8-ounces) Cheddar cheese, shredded

Cook pasta according to package directions, rinse and drain. Meanwhile, brown ground beef and onion; drain. Add spaghetti sauce and heat through. Combine the cheese. and set aside. Layer in a sprayed slow cooker using half pasta, meat sauce and cheese. Repeat layers, ending with cheese. Cover and cook on LOW 2½ to 3 hours or until heated through. Makes 8 servings.

Chicken Fettuccine

½ cup butter, plus 3 tablespoons
1 cup heavy whipping cream
1 cup freshly grated Parmesan cheese
¼ teaspoon pepper
3 chicken breast halves, skinned, boned
8 ounces fettuccine

Place ½ cup butter, cream, Parmesan and pepper in slow cooker. Cover and cook on LOW about 45 minutes. All you really need to do here is melt and blend the ingredients together.

Meanwhile, cut chicken into bite-size pieces and cook in remaining butter in large skillet. Drain and set aside.

Cook pasta according to directions on package. Drain and add to slow cooker along with the chicken. Serve immediately, or cover and keep hot until ready to serve. Makes 4 servings.

I can't think of an easier way to make Fettuccine. The slow cooker also solves the problem of how to keep it hot while you get everything else on the table. This recipe would work well for a buffet.

Poppy Seed Noodles

8 ounces egg noodles
¼ cup butter
¾ cup frozen peas, thawed
¾ teaspoon poppy seeds
Salt and pepper

Cook egg noodles according to package directions; drain.

Meanwhile, place remaining ingredients in slow cooker. Add cooked noodles and toss to coat. Cover and keep hot on LOW heat for as long as 2 hours. Makes 6 servings.

Making the pasta ahead and keeping hot in a slow cooker will free you to do other things. Especially convenient if you have to do some last minute dishes.

Macaroni & Cheese Bake

Note: *Cook only until hot in the center and the mixture is nice and creamy. After that, the cheese may start to separate somewhat. It will still taste good, but it may not look as good.*

2½ cups (about 10-ounces) elbow macaroni
2 large eggs, lightly beaten
1 tablespoon prepared mustard
1/8 teaspoon pepper
2 cups half and half
4 cups (16-ounces) Cheddar cheese, shredded

Cook macaroni according to package directions; drain. Combine eggs, mustard, pepper and half and half. Add macaroni and then the cheese. Pour into a sprayed slow cooker. Cover and cook on HIGH 2 hours or until heated through and the cheese has melted. Stir after 1 or 1½ hours, stirring the outer edges into the center. Makes 8 servings.

Pesto Lasagna

Note: *For best flavor, the Lasagna must be thoroughly heated throughout before serving.*

8 lasagna noodles
1 large egg
1 cup dry curd cottage cheese
½ cup pesto sauce
½ cup freshly grated Parmesan cheese
3 cups (12-ounces) Mozzarella cheese, shredded

Cook pasta according to package directions; drain and rinse with cold water. Place 4 noodles in a sprayed slow cooker, cutting to fit. In a food processor or blender, combine the egg, cottage cheese, pesto sauce and Parmesan cheese. Spread over noodles. Sprinkle with 1 cup Mozzarella cheese. Top with remaining 4 noodles and sprinkle with remaining cheese. Cover and cook on LOW 3 to 3½ hours, watching carefully the last half hour. Makes 8 servings.

Vegetables

Vegetables

Vegetables take an unbelievably long time to cook in a slow cooker. They should be cut into small pieces and placed in the bottom and/or around the sides of the slow cooker.

Liquid should always be added to the pot, especially at the beginning. Remember root vegetables (such as potatoes and carrots) go under the meat and quick cooking vegetables (such as peas and corn) go on the top or can be added the last 30 minutes of cooking time.

Pasta and rice can be cooked in the slow cooker, but close attention needs to be made to the cooking times or it may overcook.

When cooking rice do not decrease the amount of water when adjusting a recipe for a slow cooker.

Pasta should be pre-cooked, but slightly undercooked before adding to a slow cooker.

Easy Barley Casserole

1	cup pearl barley
2	tablespoons butter
¾	cup chopped onion
⅓	cup slivered almonds
3	cups chicken broth

Rinse barley and drain. Melt butter in medium skillet. Add barley, onion and almonds. Cook until ingredients are lightly browned. Place in slow cooker and add chicken broth. Cover and cook on LOW 4½ to 5 hours or until barley is tender and most of the broth is absorbed. Makes 6 servings.

Hint: I have found the barley to be much more flavorful if a small amount of broth is left in the pot rather than completely absorbed.

I really should cook barley more often. This recipe is easy to prepare, quite delicious and inexpensive. You can serve it with just about anything in place of rice or potatoes.

Baked Beans & Bacon

2	cans (31-ounces each) pork and beans
½	cup packed light brown sugar
2	teaspoons dry mustard
½	cup ketchup
8	slices bacon, cooked and crumbled

Drain off most of the liquid from the top of the beans. Place in slow cooker along with the next three ingredients. Cover and cook on LOW 5 to 6 hours. If beans are more liquid than you like, cook on HIGH for an additional hour. Add bacon the last 30 minutes of cooking time. Makes 8 to 10 servings.

I think baked beans were made to be cooked in a slow cooker. It is ideal for cooking in quantities and for keeping the beans warm.

Navy Bean Baked Beans

1   package (16-ounces) dried navy beans
1   cup finely chopped onion
1   cup packed light brown sugar
1   cup ketchup
1   tablespoon prepared mustard
1   can (8-ounces) crushed pineapple, with juice

Rinse and sort beans. Place in a slow cooker and add 8 cups water. Cover and cook on LOW 10 to 12 hours or until beans are tender.

Drain beans, then return to a sprayed slow cooker. Add remaining ingredients and mix well. Cover and cook on LOW 8 to 10 hours or until flavors have blended and mixture has thickened. Makes about 8 servings.

Note: Even finely chopped, the onions may not cook through. To eliminate this problem, you can pre-cook the onion in a small amount of water in the microwave. If desired, put the beans on the night before and let them cook all night. Then combine with the remaining ingredients and cook all day.

Variation: The crushed pineapple can be omitted, but it does add a lot of favor. If desired, add cooked crumbled bacon, sliced hot dogs or Little Smokies.

Pinto Beans

2 cups dried pinto beans
Salt and pepper to taste

Rinse and sort beans. Place in a slow cooker and add water to 2-inches above the beans. Cover and cook on LOW 7 to 8 hours or until tender. Watch carefully after about 6 hours. You don't want to overcook the beans. Salt and pepper to taste. Makes 5 cups cooked beans.
How to Use: *As a vegetable, it is one way to get your fiber. Use to make refried beans or a bean dip. Also great in casseroles, soups, salads and beans and rice.*

Green Bean Casserole

3   cans (14-ounces each) green beans, drained
1   can (10¾-ounces) condensed Cream of Mushroom soup
2   tablespoons milk
1   teaspoon light soy sauce
2   tablespoons slivered almonds
¾   cup (3-ounces) Cheddar cheese, shredded (optional)

This is a variation of a very old recipe developed by the Campbell® Soup Company. It graces more tables during the holidays than probably any other vegetable recipe.

Place green beans in a sprayed slow cooker. In a small bowl, combine soup, milk and soy sauce; add almonds. Pour over green beans and toss to coat. Cover and cook on LOW 5 to 5½ hours. Sprinkle cheese over top last half hour of cooking time. Makes 6 servings.

Variation: Add mushrooms or cooked bacon bits. Chopped oil-packed sun-dried tomatoes would be very good too.

Yams or Sweet Potatoes?

Yams and sweet potatoes are very similar and quite confusing to most shoppers as the names are often used interchangeably. Yams are often called sweet potatoes, but are rarely grown in the United States. In the Southern states sweet potatoes may be called Yams and canned Sweet Potatoes are often called Yams. Whatever they are called, I prefer the ones with a darker skin and an orange flesh. They are sweeter, and I think, have more flavor.

Cheesy Green Bean Casserole

Cooking this casserole in a slow cooker will free up your oven for other things. Serve the beans from the cooker or place in a serving dish and serve. Very good reheated.

3   cans (14-ounces each) green beans, drained
¾   cup finely chopped onion
2   tablespoons butter, melted
2   tablespoons flour
½   teaspoon salt
2   cups (8-ounces) Monterey Jack cheese, shredded

Place green beans and onion in a sprayed slow cooker. Combine butter and flour and toss with beans. Add salt and cheese and toss thoroughly to mix. Cover and cook on HIGH 3 to 3½ hours or until cheese is melted and beans are heated through, stirring ingredients half way through cooking time, if possible. Makes about 8 servings.

Note: It is possible to overcook this recipe. Watch carefully the last hour of cooking time.

Green Bean Dish

Variation: My family doesn't like tomatoes added to this dish, but I like to top the beans with 3 to 4 tomato slices and then the sauce.

3   cans (14-ounces each) green beans, drained
½   cup finely chopped onion
½   butter
4   teaspoons prepared mustard
2   teaspoons prepared horseradish
2   tablespoons packed light brown sugar

Place green beans in a slow cooker. Combine remaining ingredients in a small heavy saucepan and cook until onions are soft; pour over green beans. Cover and cook on LOW 2½ to 3 hours. Makes 6 servings.

Company Carrots

3 pounds carrots, sliced diagonally into ½-inch slices
¼ cup packed light brown sugar
1 teaspoon salt (optional)
½ teaspoon cracked black pepper
½ cup butter, sliced

Place carrots in slow cooker. Sprinkle with brown sugar, salt and pepper. Distribute butter slices over top. Cover and cook on HIGH 4 to 5 hours. Stir carrots half way through cooking time. Watch carefully the last hour to ensure desired amount of doneness. Makes 8 servings.

The slow cooker is a great way to cook carrots for a crowd. Just make sure you allow enough time for them to cook.

Carrots & Apricot

Desired number of carrots, julienned
Apricot preserves
¼ teaspoon salt (optional)

Place carrots in a slow cooker and add about a cup of water. Cover and cook on LOW 8 to 10 hours or until tender. Drain thoroughly and toss with the salt and just enough apricot preserves to lightly coat. It doesn't take that much, so add sparingly at first.

Carrots can take forever to cook in a slow cooker. You can reduce the time greatly by cutting the carrots into julienned pieces (narrow strips) and cooking on HIGH.

Corn Pudding

Every cookbook should have a good corn pudding recipe.

1/3 cup sugar
1/4 cup flour
3/4 teaspoon salt
4 large eggs, lightly beaten
2 cups milk
4 cups frozen corn, thawed

Combine sugar, flour and salt in a sprayed slow cooker. Combine eggs and milk and gradually stir into flour mixture. Add corn; cover and cook on HIGH 5 to 6 hours or until custard is set. Makes 6 servings.

Swiss Corn Casserole

Must be served hot, as the cheese has a tendency to cool off really fast and separate somewhat from the corn. It doesn't affect the taste, but it will not be quite as smooth.

3 cups frozen corn, thawed
1½ cups (6-ounces) Swiss cheese, shredded
1 cup heavy cream
2 large eggs, lightly beaten
Dash pepper

Combine all the ingredients in a sprayed slow cooker, mixing well. Cover and cook on LOW 2½ to 3 hours or until set in the center. Serve right away or keep hot until serving time. Makes 6 servings.

Green Peas Deluxe

1   package (32-ounces) frozen peas, do not thaw
1   teaspoon salt, or to taste
1/8   teaspoon black pepper
1   tablespoon sugar
¼   cup butter

Place peas in a slow cooker. Sprinkle with salt, pepper and sugar. Dot with butter. Cover and cook on LOW 3 to 3½ hours or until peas are thawed and heated through. Stir before serving. Makes 10 to 12 servings.

Note: Don't overcook or the peas will have that wrinkled look.

Variation: Add 1 can sliced water chestnuts; if too large, cut in halves or fourths. Or add diced pimientos.

Garlic Butter Red Potatoes

12   small red potatoes, should be uniform is size
2   tablespoons olive oil
Butter, melted
Garlic salt
Pepper

Wash potatoes (do not dry) and place in slow cooker. Add olive oil and toss to coat. Cover and cook on LOW 9 to 10 hours or until potatoes are tender, or cook on HIGH to speed up the cooking time.

Remove potatoes and cut in half. Return to slow cooker and add the butter, garlic salt and pepper. Toss to coat. Makes 4 servings.

Variation: If desired, cook minced garlic in the butter, cooking over low heat just until soft. Toss with the potatoes. Omit garlic salt and add salt and pepper to taste.

Baked Potatoes

You don't need to heat up the oven for just four potatoes as the slow cooker makes a great substitute.

4   medium baking potatoes
   Choice of toppings

Wash potatoes, but do not dry. Place in slow cooker in one layer. (If using more potatoes, stand them on end, so each one is touching the bottom.) Cover and cook on LOW 7 to 8 hours or until cooked through. Makes 4 servings.

Hint: Potatoes can be layered, but the top layer will take longer to cook. Rotating the layers occasionally will help, but still may take a little longer to cook.

Creamy Potato Dish

These come out almost like mashed potatoes.

1   package (30-ounces) frozen shredded hash browns
2   cups heavy whipping cream
¼   cup butter, melted
   Salt and pepper, desired amount
½   cup freshly grated Parmesan cheese

Place partially thawed hash browns in a sprayed slow cooker. Combine cream, butter, salt and pepper and pour over the top; it won't quite cover the potatoes, but the potatoes will cook down. Cover and cook on HIGH 3 hours or until most of the liquid is absorbed. Sprinkle with cheese and cook 45 minutes to an hour or until cheese is melted and casserole starts to brown around the edges. Makes 8 servings.

Baked Potato Casserole

4½ pounds baking potatoes, about 6 large (8 to 9 cups, cooked and cubed)
4 ounces Canadian bacon slices, diced
2 cups sour cream
1 can (10¾-ounces) condensed Cream of Chicken soup
⅓ cup green onions, green part
3 cups (12-ounces) Cheddar cheese, shredded

Bake potatoes in oven; let cool. Cut into bite-size cubes and place in a sprayed slow cooker. Combine Canadian bacon, sour cream and soup. Add onion and cheese. Pour over potatoes and stir gently to mix. Cover and cook on HIGH 4 to 5 hours or until heated through and the cheese has melted. Makes 10 to 12 servings.

Note: You can overcook this casserole, in which case, it tends to become liquid and separate. If it has to wait too long, spoon into a casserole and reheat in oven when ready to serve.

Sweet Potatoes with Marshmallows

2 cans (2 pounds 8 ounces each) canned sweet potatoes, drained
⅓ cup butter
¾ cup packed light brown sugar
Large marshmallows

Place sweet potatoes in a sprayed slow cooker. Dot small pieces butter over potatoes. Sprinkle brown sugar over top. Cover and cook on HIGH 3 to 3½ hours.

During last 20 minutes of cooking time, arrange marshmallows over potatoes to cover. Cook until soft and somewhat puffy. Do not cook beyond this point or they will turn to liquid. Makes 6 to 8 servings.

If you don't have enough oven space for the sweet potatoes, use your slow cooker. The liquid doesn't get quite as thick and the marshmallows won't brown, but it is still very good.

Apple & Sweet Potato Casserole

If desired, substitute 2 cans (2 pounds 8 ounces each) sweet potatoes for the fresh sweet potatoes. This makes a large recipe that will go well with your Thanksgiving or Christmas dinner. Reduce heat to LOW if you aren't quite ready to serve.

6	medium sweet potatoes, cooked and peeled
6	Granny Smith apples
½	cup butter
1	cup sugar
5	tablespoons cornstarch

Cut sweet potatoes into ½-inch slices. Peel apples and cut into ½-inch slices. Layer in sprayed slow cooker, starting with apples and ending with potatoes.

Meanwhile, combine butter and 2 cups water in a medium saucepan; bring to a boil. Combine sugar and cornstarch. Add to water mixture, stirring until blended. Bring back to a boil, stirring constantly. At this point, it should be thickened. Pour over apples and sweet potatoes. Cover and cook on HIGH 4 to 4½ hours or until apples are tender. Makes 10 to 12 servings.

Note: There may be quite a bit of liquid in the pot and you may wish to drain off a small amount.

Creamy Lemon Rice

Variation: Omit the cream and you will have a nice light lemon flavored rice.

1	cup uncooked long-grain rice
¼	cup butter, melted
2	teaspoons fresh lemon zest
2	cups chicken broth
½	cup heavy cream

Combine all the ingredients in a sprayed slow cooker. Cover and cook on LOW 4 to 5 hours or until liquid is absorbed and rice is tender. Makes 6 servings.

Cheesy Rice Casserole

1¾	cups uncooked long-grain rice
1⅓	cups finely chopped onion
2	cans (14-ounces each) canned chicken broth
⅓	cup sliced almonds
1½	cups (6-ounces) Cheddar cheese, shredded

Combine all the ingredients in a sprayed slow cooker. Cover and cook on LOW 3½ to 4 hours or until liquid is absorbed and rice is tender. Makes 8 servings.

Broccoli Rice Casserole

2	boxes (7.2-ounces each) chicken flavored rice vermicelli mix
1	package (16-ounces) frozen chopped broccoli, thawed
2	cans (10¾-ounces each) condensed Cream of Chicken soup
8	ounces process cheese spread, cubed
2	to 3 tablespoons sliced almonds

Cook rice mix according to package directions, cooking until tender, but not soft.

Meanwhile, combine broccoli, soup and cheese in a sprayed slow cooker. Add rice mixture and gently stir to mix. Cover and cook on HIGH 2½ to 3 hours. Sprinkle with almonds last ½ hour of cooking time. Makes about 12 servings.

Note: In order to cook through, the onion needs to be very finely chopped. If possible, try to stir the rice midway through cooking time, since it tends to cook much faster around the outer edge than in the center.

This is an excellent vegetable dish for those large company or holiday dinners. You don't have to make it at the last minute and, if desired, it can be kept warm and served from the slow cooker.

Wild Rice & Cheese Casserole

A lot of flavor is packed into these six ingredients. It can also be turned into a main dish with the addition of cooked cubed chicken or ground beef.

2	packages (6-ounces each) Long-grain and Wild Rice with seasoning packet
1½	cups chopped onion
1	cup chopped celery
½	cup butter, melted
8	ounces process cheese spread, cubed
1	can (10¾-ounces) condensed Cream of Mushroom soup

Place first 5 ingredients in sprayed slow cooker.

Place soup in a medium mixing bowl and gradually add 1 cup water, whisking until smooth. Add to rice mixture along with 2 cups water. Cover and cook on LOW 4 to 5 hours or until onion is soft and liquid is absorbed. Mixture will still be quite moist. If rice starts to brown around the edges, stir once or twice during cooking time. Makes 8 to 10 servings.

Acorn Squash

2   small acorn squash
Salt and pepper
Butter

Cut squash in half lengthwise; remove seeds. Rinse with water (don't dry) and place, cut side up in slow cooker. Sprinkle lightly with salt and pepper. Cover and cook on LOW 2 to 3 hours depending on size. Remove and place a thin slice of butter in each center. Makes 4 servings.

This recipe is so easy to do in a slow cooker. Also, try experimenting with some of your favorite recipes.

VARIATIONS:

• Dot with butter and brown sugar and cook until melted.

• Fill with cooked apples and pears. Sprinkle lightly with nutmeg.

• Fill with hot buttered peas.

Note

Acorn squash can sometimes be very hard to cut. With a heavy sharp knife, carefully pierce squash deeply in 2 or 3 places. Place in microwave and heat for 1 minute. The squash should feel slightly warm. Then cut in half. It works every time.

Zucchini Casserole

Note: *A lot of liquid will accumulate in the bottom of the pot. I would suggest removing the vegetables to serve rather than serving from the pot. This delightful vegetable dish makes a lot. If desired, you can reduce the recipe by half. You can also substitute Cheddar cheese for the Monterey Jack.*

4   medium zucchini
Salt and pepper
1   medium onion, thinly sliced
1   medium green pepper, thinly sliced
6   plum tomatoes, sliced crosswise into ¼-inch slices
1½ cups (6-ounces) Monterey Jack cheese with peppers

Cut zucchini into slices about ½-inch thick. Place in a sprayed slow cooker. Sprinkle with salt and pepper.

Layer onions, green pepper and then the tomatoes, sprinkling each layer with salt and pepper. Cover and cook on LOW 5 to 6 hours or until vegetables are almost tender. Sprinkle with cheese, cover and cook until vegetables are tender and cheese has melted—about 30 minutes. Makes 8 to 10 servings.

Fajita Vegetable Mixture

Add cooked beef or chicken and serve in flour tortillas. The mixture is also good served over grilled steaks or hamburgers or as a vegetable wrap rolled in flour tortillas.

2   large sweet peppers, 1 red and 1 green julienned
3   large onions, thinly sliced and separated
2   tablespoons olive oil
½   teaspoon paprika
Salt and pepper to taste

Place ingredients in a slow cooker and toss to mix well. Cover and cook on HIGH 3½ to 4 hours or until vegetables are crisp tender. Makes 2 to 3 cups.

Desserts & Sauces

Slow Cooker Desserts

*T*he slow cooker is ideal for certain fruits, puddings, custards and jams with some recipes working better than others. It is sometimes difficult to pass up sweets, but fresh fruit desserts make an ideal low fat treat at the end of a meal.

The few cakes and fruit crisps I have tried in my slow cooker have been less that satisfactory for my taste, yet I have had people tell me they enjoy making these recipes.

Do try the Pear & Pineapple Chutney on page 155, the Chocolate and Caramel sauce and the Chunky Applesauce. These are nice make ahead recipes that are convenient to have on hand.

Bev's Bread Pudding

8 cups cubed raisin bread (approximately 12 slices)
4 large eggs
¼ cup sugar
2 cups whole milk
¼ cup butter, melted
½ teaspoon cinnamon

Place bread cubes in a sprayed slow cooker.

Combine eggs, sugar and milk. Add butter and cinnamon. Pour over bread cubes. Press the bread down into the milk until soaked, then fluff up a little with a fork. Cover and bake on LOW 2 to 3 hours or until the pudding is somewhat firm, but still soft. Makes 6 servings.

This is an adaptation of a recipe Bev sent to me. You can serve the pudding warm with whipped cream or with ice cream. Or, as Bev does, with the vanilla sauce:

Vanilla Sauce

2 tablespoons butter
2 tablespoons flour
¾ cup sugar
1 teaspoon vanilla extract

Melt butter in a medium saucepan. Add flour and stir with a whisk until smooth. Add sugar and vanilla along with 1 cup water. Bring to a boil, stirring frequently until thickened.

Baked Apples

You can use baking apples other than Golden Delicious, but I have found the Granny Smiths take a little longer to cook.

4	Golden Delicious apples
1	cup apple cider
¼	cup butter
1	can (14-ounces) sweetened condensed milk
1/3	cup chopped pecans
1	teaspoon rum extract

Core apples (do not peel) and place in slow cooker. Add apple cider and cook on LOW 3½ to 4 hours or until apples are tender. Test for doneness with the thin blade of a sharp knife. Makes 4 servings.

Meanwhile, melt butter in a small saucepan. Add remaining ingredients and cook over medium heat, stirring constantly, until mixture is smooth and creamy, about 8 to 10 minutes. Sauce will thicken as it cools. Reheat the sauce when ready to serve with the apples. Makes 1½ cups sauce.

Peaches & Ice Cream

The sauce makes a nice gift packaged in a decorative jar. Make sure you include the cinnamon sticks for added color. The longer the cinnamon sticks stay in the peaches, the stronger the flavor.

2	cans (15-ounces each) sliced peaches with juice
1	can (15-ounces) apricot halves, drained
2	tablespoons fresh lemon juice
2	4-inch cinnamon sticks
	Vanilla ice cream

Add peaches, apricot halves, lemon juice and cinnamon sticks to a slow cooker. Cover and cook on LOW 2 to 3 hours or until heated through. Allow to cool and store in refrigerator until ready to use. Serve over ice cream. Makes 3½ cups.

Cranberry-Pear Dish

4	pears, halved, peeled and cored
1	cup fresh or frozen cranberries
6	thin lemon slices
1	cup sugar
¼	teaspoon cinnamon
1/8	teaspoon cloves

Place pears, cut-side down, in a sprayed slow cooker. Add cranberries and lemon slices.

In small saucepan, combine sugar, cinnamon and cloves with ½ cup water. Bring to a boil and cook until sugar is dissolved. Pour over fruit. Cover and cook on LOW 4½ to 5 hours or until pears are tender. Half way through cooking time, turn pears, cut-side up and make sure the cranberries are covered with liquid. Makes 4 to 8 servings.

The pears can be served warm or room temperature. Serve with pork roast, pork chops or ham. Or serve as a dessert with whipped cream or ice cream.

Patrick's Easy Fudge

2	cups semi-sweet chocolate chips
1	square (1-ounce) unsweetened chocolate, coarsely chopped
1	can (14-ounces) sweetened condensed milk
1	teaspoon vanilla extract
1½	cups chopped pecans or walnuts

Place chocolate chips, chocolate square and condensed milk in a lightly sprayed slow cooker. Cover and cook on LOW 1 to 1½ hours or until chocolate has melted.

Add vanilla and stir to blend. Add nuts and pour into a lightly buttered 9x9-inch baking dish. Cover and chill until firm. Makes 36 pieces.

A very good fudge with the taste of dark chocolate. What you are basically doing here is using your slow cooker to melt the chocolate. My grandson Patrick feels like he is making fudge all by himself when he adds the ingredients to the slow cooker.

Apple Butter

I'm not really a fan of apple butter, but I do have to admit this is quite delicious. I used Braeburn apples. But Granny Smith or Golden Delicious would also be good.

6 pounds (about 12) cooking apples, peeled, cored and sliced
5 cups sugar
1 cup packed light brown sugar
¾ cup full-flavored apple cider
1 teaspoon nutmeg
1 teaspoon cinnamon

Place all the ingredients in a very large mixing bowl and toss well to combine. Spoon into a sprayed slow cooker; cover and cook on LOW 7 to 8 hours or until apples are tender.

Remove apples from the liquid and place in a large bowl; discard liquid. Mash the apples and return to the pot. Cover and cook on LOW 2 to 2½ hours or until mixture is thick. If desired, mash any remaining pieces of apple. Cover and store in refrigerator. Will keep about 3 weeks. Makes about 4 cups.

Note: The mixture should be thick, but bear in mind that it will thicken more as it cools.

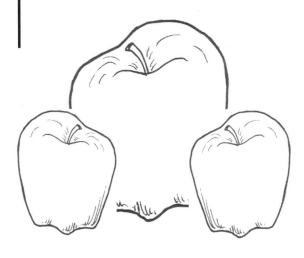

Pear & Pineapple Chutney

8 cups pears, peeled, cored and coarsely chopped
1 can (20-ounces) crushed pineapple, well drained
2 cups sugar

Combine ingredients and mix well. Place in a sprayed slow cooker. Cover and cook on HIGH 3 to 4 hours or until pears are tender, but not mushy. Remove from pot with a slotted spoon. This removes most of the excess liquid, but leaves some in the chutney. Makes about 5 cups.

What an easy way to make a delicious accompaniment to ham. This would also be delicious drained and served on hot rolls, or not too sweet muffins. If you can bear to part with it, pour into attractive jars, add decorated lids and give as a gift or include as an addition to a gift basket.

Note: The pears shouldn't be chopped too small; the size of a pineapple tidbit is just about right.

Noodle Pudding

16 ounces egg noodles
½ cup butter, cubed
1 cup sugar
10 large eggs, lightly beaten
¾ cup milk

Cook pasta according to package directions; drain. Place in a large sprayed slow cooker; add butter and toss until melted.

Combine sugar, eggs and milk. Pour over pasta and stir to mix. Cover and cook on LOW 3½ to 4 hours or until set. Makes about 12 servings.

Variation: For a sweeter version, add raisins before cooking, or serve with a small amount of jam or preserves.

I make this dish in my 5 quart oval-shaped slow cooker. If you don't have an oval pot, the pudding may be thicker, which is fine, just cut into narrow slices instead of squares.

Peachy Fruit Sauce

*Serve this deli-
cious sauce over
ice cream, pound
cake or cheese-
cake.*

2   packages (16-ounces each) frozen sliced peaches
1   package (12-ounces) frozen raspberries
1   cup sugar
1   cup frozen blueberries

Partially thaw peaches and cut each slice in half crosswise. Place in a sprayed slow cooker along with the raspberries and sugar. Cover and cook on HIGH 2 hours. Add
frozen blueberries and cook 30 minutes. Makes 6 cups.

Pink & Chunky Applesauce

5   golden delicious apples
2   tablespoons apple juice or water
¼   cup sugar
½   cup cherry preserves

Peel and core apples. Cut into ¼ to ½ inch slices and
place in a sprayed slow cooker. Add apple juice and
sugar, tossing to coat. Cover and cook on Low 6 to 7
hours or until apples are just tender.

Stir in the cherry preserves, crushing some
of the apples if they are too large. Makes 3 cups.

Chunky Applesauce

5   large Golden Delicious apples
5   large Rome apples
¾   cup sugar
½   teaspoon cinnamon
¼   teaspoon ground ginger
5   large strips of fresh orange peel

Peel, slice and core apples. Cut into ¼ to ½-inch slices. You should have about 12 cups. Place in slow cooker along with remaining ingredients and ¼ cup water. Cover and cook on LOW 8 to 10 hours, stirring about every 2 hours. When done, apples should be soft, but not mushy. Remove orange peel and discard. Makes 5 to 6 cups.

Hint:

Cooking time can vary according to the types of apples used, ripeness and moisture content. If you are ready for the applesauce, but it isn't ready for you, you can speed things up by cooking on HIGH or place in a large stock pot and cook until soft.

Chocolate Sauce

2   cups heavy whipping cream
2   cups (12-ounces) semi-sweet chocolate chips

Place ingredients in a slow cooker. Cover and cook on LOW 2½ to 3 hours. Stir until smooth. Pour into a glass jar; cover and chill. Mixture will thicken as it cools. Makes about 2½ cups.

Note: Since there is a relatively small quantity of ingredients, use a 3½ quart or smaller slow cooker, if you have one.

Deliciously Easy Caramel Dip

You will keep going back for more with this easy recipe. Serve to your guest as a "fondue dessert" with sliced apples, pears, strawberries, banana chunks and pound cake cubes or serve over ice cream or ice cream sundaes.

1   cup packed light brown sugar
½   cup light corn syrup
1   can (14-ounces) sweetened condensed milk

Combine ingredients in a sprayed slow cooker, mixing until smooth. Cook, uncovered, on HIGH 2 to 3 hours, stirring occasionally. Makes 2 cups.

Tip: If desired, add 1 teaspoon vanilla extract. Can be made ahead and chilled. Mixture will become quite firm, but can be reheated in a slow cooker, saucepan or microwave. If reheating in the microwave, watch carefully to prevent overheating.

Note: If using a slow cooker larger than 3½ quarts, I would suggest at least doubling the recipe.

A Little Something Extra

Lagniappe

Pronunciation: lăn-yăp`

Etymology: (1844) American French, from American Spanish. Chiefly Southern Louisiana & Mississippi

1. A small gift given to a customer by a merchant at the time of purchase.

2. An extra or unexpected gift or benefit.

This chapter is my lagniappe to you. The remaining section of this book contains more wonderful Six Ingredients or Less recipes you can make and enjoy along with the delicious slow cooker recipes. A little bit of this and that, some old favorites and some new is my gift to you.

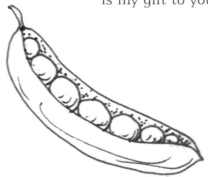

Garlic Cheese Bread

1 large garlic clove, peeled
½ cup butter, softened slightly
2 tablespoons shredded Cheddar cheese
2 tablespoons freshly grated Parmesan cheese
1 loaf French bread, sliced in half lengthwise

Delicious is the only way to describe this bread. Butter, garlic and cheese - Yum!

Place garlic in a small food processor or blender and process until minced. Add butter, Cheddar and Parmesan cheese. Process until blended and smooth. Spread on bread, but not too thick. Place on a baking sheet and bake at 450° for 4 to 5 minutes or until heated through and just beginning to crisp (top should not be brown). Cut into diagonal slices and serve. About 12 servings.

Cheesy Poppy Seed Bread

8 1-inch slices French bread
1/3 cup butter, softened
½ cup freshly grated Parmesan cheese
1 teaspoon poppy seeds

Combine butter, cheese and poppy seeds. Spread mixture on one side of bread slices. Place on a baking sheet and bake at 325° for 10 to 12 minutes or until lightly toasted. Makes 8 servings.

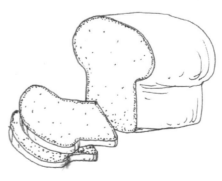

Tomato & Cheese Melts

These are wonderful served as a snack or as an accompaniment to a soup or salad. For additional color, place a small basil leaf on the cheese or sprinkle with parsley.

4   slices French bread, about ¾-inch thick
Olive Oil
Thin slices of tomato, cut to fit bread
Garlic salt
Freshly grated Parmesan cheese
4   thin slices Mozzarella cheese

Place bread slices on a baking sheet and brush lightly with olive oil. Place under broiler and broil until lightly toasted.

Turn bread over and arrange 1 layer of tomato slices over top. Sprinkle lightly with garlic salt and Parmesan. Cover with a cheese slice. Place under broiler and broil until heated through and cheese is melted. Makes 4 servings.

Sally Lunn Bread

A delicious light muffin type bread. Can be served with fresh fruit for a light dessert.

½   cup butter, softened
1   cup sugar
2   large eggs
2   cups flour
1   tablespoon baking powder
1   cup milk

In a mixer bowl, cream the butter and sugar. Add eggs and mix thoroughly. Combine flour and baking powder and add to butter mixture alternately with the milk, starting and ending with the flour. Pour into a sprayed 9x5-inch loaf pan and bake at 400° for 40 to 45 minutes or until tester inserted in center comes out clean. Turn out on rack and serve warm. Makes 1 loaf.

Flaky Biscuits

2 cups flour
½ teaspoon salt
2 teaspoons sugar
1 tablespoon plus 1 teaspoon baking powder
½ cup shortening
2/3 cup milk

In a mixing bowl, combine the flour, salt, sugar and baking powder. Cut in the shortening with a pastry blender or fork until mixture is about the size of small peas. Add milk and stir just until mixture forms a ball.

Place dough on a lightly floured board and gently knead about 12 times or until dough is smooth. Here again, you want to handle gently and not overmix. Pat into a ½ inch thick circle and with a 2½ inch cookie cutter, cut into about 16 biscuits. Place about 1 inch apart on a lightly sprayed shallow baking pan and bake at 425° for 12 to 15 minutes or until lightly browned and cooked through.

Quick Bran Muffins

2 cups Bran Flakes
1 cup baking mix
½ cup sugar
1 large egg, lightly beaten
½ cup milk
¼ cup vegetable oil

Place Bran Flakes and baking mix in a mixing bowl. Combine remaining ingredients and add to above mixture, mixing to blend. Spoon into a well-greased 6 cup muffin tin. Bake at 400° for 18 to 20 minutes or until a tester inserted in center comes out clean. Makes 6 muffins.

I don't know how many biscuit recipes I have tried over the years, but this is the one I seem to make most often.

Note: Many recipes call for 2 inch cookie cutters, which is okay, but if you are a true biscuit fan, you will probably want to make larger biscuits. Or, you can pat the dough into a rectangle rather than a circle and cut into desired size squares.

Note: The muffin tin I used measured 3 inches across the top, and when baked, the muffins overflowed somewhat, creating that crunchy top many of us like.

Sour Cream Muffins

Muffins are almost always best served right out of the oven and these are no exception. These flavorful muffins are slightly sweet with a nice crunch.

2	cups flour
½	cup sugar
3	teaspoons baking powder
½	cup butter, chilled and cubed
2	large eggs, lightly beaten
½	cup sour cream

Combine the flour, sugar and baking powder in a mixing bowl. Cut in the butter with a pastry blender or fork until mixture resembles small peas. Add eggs and sour cream and stir until the flour is moistened; the batter will be quite stiff.

Spoon into sprayed muffin tins filling about two-thirds full. Bake at 425° for 18 to 20 minutes or until lightly browned and a tester inserted in center comes out clean. Makes 12 muffins.

Biscuit Muffins

Crunchy on the outside. Soft in the middle. Delicious!

Hint: *If using dark gray or black muffin tins, decrease oven temperature by 25°.*

2	cups flour
2½	teaspoons baking powder
¾	teaspoon salt
½	cup cold butter, cubed
1	large egg, lightly beaten
¾	cup milk

In a large mixing bowl, combine the flour, baking powder and salt. Cut in the butter with a pastry blender or a fork. Combine egg and milk; stir to mix. Add to flour mixture and mix just until flour is moistened. Spoon into a sprayed muffin tin, filling about two-thirds full. Bake at 425° for 18 to 20 minutes or until lightly browned and tester inserted in center comes out clean. Makes 11 to 12 muffins.

Lemon Poppyseed Muffins

- 1 package (16-ounces) Pound Cake mix
- 1 cup sour cream
- 2 large eggs
- 1 tablespoon poppy seeds
- 1 tablespoon freshly grated lemon zest
- 1 teaspoon lemon extract

Combine all the ingredients in a mixer bowl. Beat on medium speed about 2 minutes or until well blended and smooth. Spoon into 12 sprayed muffin cups, filling a little more than half full. Bake at 325° for 20 to 30 minutes or until tester inserted in center comes out clean. Carefully remove from pan and let cool or serve warm. Makes 12 muffins.

Herb Popovers

- 2 large eggs
- 1 cup flour
- ½ teaspoon salt
- 1 cup milk
- 4½ teaspoons butter
- 1 container (4-ounces) Garlic with Herb cheese, softened

In a mixer bowl, combine eggs, flour, salt and milk. Beat until well blended (may still be a little lumpy). Put ½ teaspoon butter in each of nine 2½-inch muffin tins. Place in oven to melt butter. Remove from oven and brush inside of tins with the butter to coat. Fill one-third full with batter. Top with 1 teaspoon of the cheese. Pour remaining batter over top, filling about two-thirds full. Bake at 425° for 25 to 30 minutes or until puffed and golden brown. Serve immediately. Makes 9 popovers.

A delightful crunchy outside with an out-of-this-world flavor! Time the popovers so they can be served immediately.

Tip: Leftover herb cheese can be served with crackers as a snack or for additional popovers.

Indian Fry Bread

Fry Bread reminds me a little bit of elephant ears, but in my opinion, is better and more versatile. Some recipes call for yeast, but this baking powder dough is much easier to make.

2¼ cups flour
2 teaspoons baking powder
1 teaspoon salt
2 tablespoons shortening, divided (melt 1 tablespoon and set aside to cool)
Oil for frying
Cinnamon sugar

Combine flour, baking powder and salt. Add 1 tablespoon shortening and cut in with a fork. Add about ¾ cup warm water, a little at a time, until dough can be formed into a ball. Place on a lightly floured surface and knead briefly until smooth. Divide into 6 pieces and roll into balls. Brush all over with the melted shortening and let stand 45 minutes.

Roll each ball into a 5 inch circle or oval. Cut a 1½-inch slit in the middle. Cook in about ¼ to ½ inch of oil heated to 360° in a deep skillet or pot, cooking one at a time. Cook until golden, about 1 minute per side. Remove and drain on paper towels. Sprinkle immediately with cinnamon sugar. Enjoy! Makes 6 large fry breads.

Variation: You can play around with this recipe and make it the way you want it. The 5 inch circles will make rounds that are nice and crisp. If you want yours more "bready", roll out thicker and smaller circles or ovals. Serve with jam or spread with butter as a bread course. You can also top the rounds with a taco salad or with hot chili and cheese.

Breakfast Puffs

½ cup butter
1 cup water
1 cup flour
4 large eggs
$^1/_3$ cup very finely chopped or cubed ham
½ cup (2-ounces) Swiss cheese, shredded

In medium saucepan, bring butter and water to a boil. Add flour and stir vigorously until mixture forms a ball, less than one minute. Remove from heat. Add eggs, one at a time, beating thoroughly each time to blend. Let cool slightly; stir in ham and cheese. Drop heaping table-spoons onto ungreased baking sheet, about 2 inches apart. Bake at 400° for 40 to 50 minutes or until puffed, lightly browned and dry. Makes 18 medium cream puffs.

Tip: For an hors d'oeuvres tray, make tiny walnut size cream puffs. Bake about 25 to 30 minutes.

A delicious cream puff with ham and Swiss cheese. Nice for breakfast, snacks, soups, or salads.

Parmesan Sticks

1 loaf unsliced French or Italian bread
1 cup butter, melted
¼ cup freshly grated Parmesan cheese

Cut bread into 1-inch slices; remove crusts. Cut into 1-inch wide strips.

Combine melted butter and cheese. Brush over all sides of the bread. Place on an ungreased baking sheet and bake at 325° for 15 to 20 minutes or until lightly toasted.

Note: The amount of butter-cheese mixture needed may vary according to the size of the loaf of bread.

The bread sticks are delicious as a bread accompaniment to dinner or served with spaghetti, lasagna, soup or salad.

Corn Bread Sticks

1   can (8.75-ounces) cream corn
2   cups baking mix
2   tablespoons butter, melted
    Parmesan cheese

Combine corn and baking mix; it will be a little moist. Turn out onto a floured surface and knead no more than 8 to 10 times using more flour as needed. Pat into a 10x6-inch rectangle. Cut lengthwise in half, then crosswise into 10 strips. Carefully place bread on a sprayed baking pan, about 1-inch apart. Brush with butter and sprinkle with a little Parmesan cheese. Bake at 450° for 10 to 12 minutes or until lightly browned and cooked through. Make 20 sticks.

Rosemary Batter Bread

How Much Flour?

Ever wonder why you may need more or less flour than called for in the recipe? A lot depends on the brand of flour used, how old it is and the humidity. If it is raining, you will probably need more flour.

3   cups all-purpose flour, divided
1   teaspoon salt
1   tablespoon sugar
2¼   teaspoons yeast or 1 package yeast
2   tablespoons shortening
1   teaspoon crushed dried rosemary leaves

In a mixer bowl, combine 2 cups of the flour, salt, sugar and yeast. Add 1¼ cups very warm water (120° to 130°), shortening and rosemary. Beat on medium speed about 2 minutes, scraping bowl frequently. By hand, stir in remaining 1 cup flour until batter is smooth. Spoon into a sprayed 9x5x3-inch loaf pan. Cover and let rise until double, about 45 to 60 minutes. Bake at 375° for 35 to 45 minutes or until bread sounds hollow when tapped on bottom. Remove and cool on rack. Makes 1 loaf.

Hearty Wheat Bread

1½	cups milk
¼	cup butter
1/3	cup light molasses
2	teaspoons salt
2¼	teaspoons yeast or 1 package yeast
5½	to 6 cups whole wheat flour

In a medium saucepan heat milk, butter, molasses and salt over low heat, just until butter is melted. Let cool to at least 110° or lukewarm.

Meanwhile, soften yeast in ½ cup warm water (105° to 110°). Let stand 5 to 10 minutes.

In a large mixer bowl, and using the paddle attachment, combine yeast and milk mixture with 4 cups flour. Add another cup of flour and beat in. Switch to hook attachment and beat, adding small amounts of flour as needed, to form a dough that pulls away from the side of the bowl and is slightly sticky to the touch. Turn out on floured board and knead a few times to form a smooth ball. Shape into a 12-inch long loaf. Place on a large lightly sprayed baking sheet, cover with a kitchen towel, and let rise until doubled, about 1½ to 2 hours.

Bake at 375° for 25 to 35 minutes or until bread sounds hollow when tapped on the bottom. Cool on rack. Makes 1 large loaf.

This is a wonderful hearty loaf of bread and with only one rise, it really speeds up the process of making it. If desired, divide dough to make two smaller loaves. Enjoy one today and freeze the other for future use.

Hint: 2¼ teaspoons bulk yeast = 1 package dry yeast

What!
Make My Own Bread?

Unfortunately, most of us have gotten away from making our own bread. It really isn't that hard, but it does take a little practice. The more you do it, the easier it gets. Life is too busy for most of us to make all our bread, but homemade rolls for special dinners are a treat loved and appreciated by all. The secret is in planning ahead. Perhaps even making the bread ahead and freezing.

Bread machines are quite popular today and very easy to use. Not all bread recipes work well in a bread machine though. Use recipes designed for them or if you have a favorite recipe, go ahead and try it. It may or may not work. For instance, I used to make my Pizza and Focaccia dough recipes by hand, but they work just as well in the bread machine. On the other hand, I have other recipes that don't work in the bread machine.

When I first started making bread, most of my bread came out heavy and damp. I was using far too much flour and I wasn't spending enough time kneading the dough. I also learned you have to make "sure" the dough has doubled in size. This can certainly result in a not so satisfactory bread.

With today's ever-rising prices, why not try your hand at bread making. Your family will love it and you will have the satisfaction of not only feeding your family good bread, but you will save money as well.

Whole Wheat Bread

2¼   teaspoons yeast   or 1 package yeast
2   tablespoons melted butter
4   cups all-purpose flour
1¹/₃   cups whole wheat flour
2   teaspoons salt

Dissolve yeast in ½ cup warm water (105°-110°). Place in mixer bowl along with the butter.

Combine flour, whole wheat flour and salt. Place 3½ cups flour mixture in mixer bowl along with 2 cups water. Beat with paddle attachment until smooth. Add enough of the remaining flour to make a soft, but not sticky dough; you may not need all the flour. Switch to hook attachment and beat until dough is smooth and clears the side of the bowl, about 4 to 5 minutes. Remove and place on a lightly floured surface, kneading just until smooth. Place in a sprayed bowl, turning to coat top. Cover and let rise about 60 minutes or until double in size.

Punch down dough. Shape into one large round and place on a large lightly sprayed baking sheet. Cover with a tea towel and let rise until double, about 30 to 45 minutes. Bake at 375° for 20 to 25 minutes or until lightly browned and bottom sounds hollow when tapped. Makes 1 large loaf.

Heavy Duty Mixers

The heavy duty mixers are wonderful for mixing yeast breads. The mixing time is much faster and it usually eliminates kneading by hand. But if you prefer, go ahead and mix and knead by hand. Actually this can be very therapeutic. You can take out your frustrations of the day by pounding (kneading) that little dough until "you" feel better. It is difficult to knead the dough too long.

White Bread

I omitted this tried and true recipe in my recently revised Six Ingredients or Less cookbook, but for the dissapointed young man who makes it on his fishing boat, I have included it here, just for him.

6¾	teaspoons yeast or 3 packages yeast
⅓	cup honey
1	tablespoon salt
8	to 8½ cups all-purpose flour, divided

1. Dissolve yeast and honey in ½ cup water (105° to 110°). Let stand about 10 minutes.

2. In a large mixing bowl, combine the salt and 5 cups flour with 3 cups hot tap water. Add yeast mixture and about 3 cups flour. Dough will be quite sticky.

3. Place on a floured surface and knead about 10 minutes or until dough is smooth and elastic, adding additional flour as needed. Place in a large sprayed bowl, turning to coat the top. Cover and let rise until doubled in size, about 60 minutes.

4. Punch down dough and divide into 4 portions. Form each into a loaf and place in sprayed 9x5-inch loaf pans. Cover and let rise until doubled in size (dough should rise slightly above the pan) about 40 to 60 minutes.

5. Bake at 350° for 30 to 45 minutes or until golden brown and bottom of bread sounds hollow when tapped. If it isn't quite ready, return to oven and continue baking.

6. Remove from pans and cool on rack. If desired, brush top with melted butter. Makes 4 loaves.

Swedish Rye Bread

2¼ teaspoons yeast or 1 package yeast
2 tablespoons honey
2 tablespoons vegetable oil
1 cup dark rye flour
1 teaspoon salt
2¾ cups all-purpose flour

You just might decide to make bread more often after you try this recipe.

Variation: *Add 2 teaspoons cara-way seeds when adding the rye flour.*

In a mixer bowl, dissolve the yeast and honey in 1¼ cups water (105°-110°). Add oil and rye flour, and with the paddle attachment, beat until smooth. Add salt and all-purpose flour and beat until well mixed. Switch to the hook attachment and beat 4 to 5 minutes or until smooth and elastic. Place dough in a sprayed large bowl; turn to coat the top. Cover and let rise in a warm place until doubled, about 45 to 60 minutes.

Punch down the dough, shape into a loaf and place in a sprayed 9x5-inch loaf pan. Loosely cover and let rise un-til doubled, about 45 to 60 minutes. Bake at 375° for 35 to 45 minutes or until browned and bottom of bread sounds hollow when tapped. It's okay to return the bread to the pan and continue baking, if necessary. Makes 1 loaf.

Yeast

I have recently discovered that yeast packages are suggesting lower temperatures for dissolving yeast than in the past. I have good luck with using 105° to 110° as a guideline, but I would suggest that you follow the directions on the package of yeast you are using. It should take 5 to 10 minutes for the yeast to dissolve. You should have a nice foam on the top.

Fantastic Egg Bread

A delicious and very easy bread recipe that also has a very professional look. You'll love the shape of the baked loaf. This is a recipe you will want to make often for family and friends.

2¼   teaspoons yeast or 1 package yeast
1¼   cups milk plus 1 teaspoon
4   to 4½ cups all-purpose flour
1   teaspoon salt
¼   cup butter, melted
1   large egg, lightly beaten, plus 1 egg yolk, beaten

Dissolve the yeast in the 1¼ cups milk (105° to 110°).

In mixer bowl, combine 4 cups flour and the salt. Add the butter, egg and yeast mixture. Beat with the paddle attachment until well mixed. Switch to the hook attachment and beat until smooth and elastic, adding more flour only if necessary. It's okay if the dough is just a tiny bit sticky. Place in a sprayed bowl and turn to coat top. Cover and let rise 45 to 60 minutes or until doubled.

Punch down dough and form into a ball. Cut off one-third of the dough and form each piece into a ball. Place the larger ball on a lightly sprayed baking sheet. Place the smaller ball on the top. Now this is where you can have some fun. Take the handle of a wooden spoon and press all the way down into the center of the two balls. This will secure the top ball of dough to the bottom dough. Using a serrated knife, cut about 8 1½-inch slits, ⅛ inch deep around the top of each ball of dough. Cover lightly and let rise until doubled, about 45 to 60 minutes.

Combine the beaten egg yolk with the 1 teaspoon milk and brush very lightly over the bread. Bake at 375° for 25 to 35 minutes or until golden brown and bottom of loaf sounds hollow when tapped. Let cool on rack. Makes 1 large loaf.

Sunshine Cake

6 large eggs, separated
1 cup sugar
1 teaspoon vanilla extract
2/3 cup flour
1 teaspoon cream of tartar
1/4 teaspoon salt

In a mixer bowl, beat the egg whites just until frothy. Gradually add the sugar and beat until stiff and glossy.

Lightly beat the egg yolks and fold into the meringue along with the vanilla. Combine the dry ingredients and gently fold into the batter. Pour into an ungreased tube or Bundt pan and bake at 350° for 35 to 45 minutes or until a tester inserted in center comes out clean. Cool completely before removing from pan. Makes about 8 servings.

This is a very old, but still popular recipe that is a cross between an Angel food cake and a pound cake. Serve glazed, with fresh fruit or with your favorite ice cream.

Coconut Pecan Cake

4 large eggs
1 box (16-ounces) light brown sugar
1/2 cup vegetable oil
2 cups baking mix
1 package (7-ounces) flaked coconut
1 cup chopped pecans or walnuts

In a mixer bowl, lightly beat the eggs. Add brown sugar and mix well. Stir in the oil. Add the baking mix, a small amount at a time and mix well. Stir in the coconut and nuts. Pour into an ungreased 13x9-inch baking pan and bake at 325° for 35 to 45 minutes or until a tester inserted in center comes out clean. Let cool slightly, cut into squares. Makes 12 to 16 servings.

Raisin Walnut Cake

Don't be put off
by the 1 cup
mayonnaise. It
actually takes
the place of eggs
and fat in the
recipe and it
makes for a
wonderfully
moist cake that
requires no
frosting.

Variation:
Substitute 1 cup
chopped dates for
the raisins. For
chocolate cake
add 6 tablespoons
(1½-ounces)
grated unsweet-
ened chocolate.

1	cup raisins
1	cup chopped walnuts
2	teaspoons baking soda
1	cup sugar
1	cup mayonnaise
2	cups flour

Combine raisins, walnuts and baking soda in a large mixing bowl. Add 1 cup hot water and set aside while measuring remaining ingredients.

Add sugar to raisin-nut mixture. Then stir in mayonnaise until blended. Stir in flour just until smooth. Pour into a lightly sprayed 13x9-inch baking dish. Bake at 350° for 25 to 30 minutes or until a tester inserted in center comes out clean. Makes 12 servings.

Blueberry Coffee Cake

2	cups flour
1	teaspoon baking powder
4	large eggs, lightly beaten
1	cup vegetable oil
1	cup sugar
1	can (21-ounces) blueberry pie filling

Combine flour and baking powder in a mixer bowl. Add next 3 ingredients and mix until smooth. Spread half the batter in a sprayed 13x9-inch baking pan; the layer will be thin. Spoon pie filling evenly over top. Pour remaining batter over top and gently spread to cover the filling. Bake at 350° for 35 to 45 minutes or until a tester inserted in center comes out clean. Serve warm. Makes 12 to 16 servings.

Easy Chocolate Chip Cake

1   package (18.25-ounces) German Chocolate cake mix
3   large eggs
1   can (21-ounces) apple pie filling
¾   cup chopped pecans, toasted
½   cup miniature semi-sweet chocolate chips

Place cake mix and eggs in large mixer bowl.

Place pie filling in a food processor and process to chop the apples; pulse on and off, but do not liquefy. Add to mixer bowl and beat at medium speed, 3 to 4 minutes. Mixture will be somewhat lighter in color. Pour into a sprayed 13x9-inch baking dish. Sprinkle with the pecans and then the chocolate chips. Bake at 350° for 30 to 40 minutes or until tester inserted in center comes out clean. Makes 12 servings.

Cake mixes are convenient for today's busy lifestyle. With a few favorite recipes you can have a delicious dessert with very little effort.

Banana Cake

1   box (18.25-ounces) Butter Recipe Golden cake mix
¼   cup vegetable oil
4   large eggs
1½   cup mashed very ripe bananas, about 3 large
¾   cup chopped walnuts

In a mixer bowl, combine cake mix, oil, eggs and 1 cup water. Beat until well mixed, about 2 to 3 minutes. Stir in the bananas and nuts. Pour into a sprayed 13x9-inch baking pan and bake at 350° for 25 to 30 minutes or until a cake tester inserted in center comes out clean. Place on rack and cool. Makes 12 to 16 servings.

A great eat-in-hand type of cake. Really doesn't need a frosting.

Mom's Orange Cake

My brothers and I loved it when Mom made this cake. We knew we were in for a special treat.

1   box (18.25-ounces) White cake mix with pudding
1   box (3-ounces) lemon jello
4   large eggs
¾   cup vegetable oil
3½ cups sifted powdered sugar
1   can (6-ounces) frozen orange juice concentrate, thawed

In a mixer bowl, combine the cake mix, jello, eggs, oil and ¾ cup water. Beat about 2 minutes or until smooth and thoroughly mixed. Pour into a deep 13x9-inch baking pan. Bake at 325° for 30 to 40 minutes or until a tester inserted in the center comes out clean. Let cool on rack 10 minutes.

Meanwhile, combine powdered sugar and orange juice and beat until smooth. When cake has cooled slightly, poke holes all the way to the bottom, using a kitchen fork or a skewer. Pour glaze over cake and spread to cover. Let cool. Makes 12 to 16 servings.

Tip: For easier mixing, make sure the orange juice concentrate has thoroughly thawed, and is at room temperature.

My Grandmother was an excellent cook and she gave me some of my very first cooking lessons. Cakes were her specialty as well as ham and country biscuits and gravy. At times I long for those days when we ate these comfort foods without any guilt whatsoever. Today we eat them anyway, but we do feel a little guilty about it.

Summer Peach Cake

1 box (18.25-ounces) Yellow cake mix
1/3 cup vegetable oil
3 large eggs
1 teaspoon vanilla extract
8 medium peaches, divided
2 tablespoons sugar plus sugar for sweetening the chopped peaches

In a mixer bowl, combine cake mix, oil, eggs, vanilla and 1 cup water. Beat until ingredients are mixed, then beat on medium-high for 2 minutes. Pour into a sprayed 10-inch springform pan.

Peel 4 of the peaches and cut in half. Place one half, rounded-side up, in center of the batter. Place remaining peaches around the batter making a circle. Sprinkle with 2 tablespoons sugar. Bake at 350° for 40 to 50 minutes or until a tester comes out clean. For accurate testing, try to test in the batter only and not a peach. (The peaches will have sunk to the bottom so this may be a little bit tricky.)

Meanwhile, peel and coarsely chop the remaining 4 peaches. Add sugar to taste. Let stand to dissolve the sugar. Cake can be served warm or room temperature with fresh peaches spooned over the top.

A very impressive cake that takes only minutes to prepare. If you would rather not use a mix, use your favorite yellow cake recipe. Substitute canned peach halves when fresh peaches are no longer available.

Variation: Omit the fresh chopped peaches and serve with ice cream, whipped cream or just a sprinkle of powdered sugar.

Chocolate Cake

This popular moist chocolate cake is perfect for a picnic or potluck dinner. The mayonnaise takes the place of the eggs and the oil in the recipe.

2	cups flour
1	cup sugar
¼	cup cocoa
2	teaspoons baking soda
1	cup mayonnaise
1	teaspoon vanilla extract

In mixer bowl, combine the flour, sugar, cocoa, and baking soda. Add mayonnaise, vanilla and 1½ cups water. Beat on medium speed about one minute or until well mixed and smooth. Pour into a sprayed 13x9-inch baking pan. Bake at 350° for 25 to 30 minutes or until a tester inserted in center comes out clean. Makes 12 servings.

Note: Frost with one of your favorite frostings or with the following recipe:

All butter is not created = equal =

If you are having problems with some of your cakes, cookies and candies not turning out the way they should, it could be the butter you are using. Experiment with different brands, until you get the desired result.

Chocolate Frosting

¼	cup milk
¼	cup butter
1	cup semi-sweet chocolate chips
1	teaspoon vanilla extract
2½	cups sifted powdered sugar

Combine milk and butter in a small saucepan. Bring to a boil then remove from heat. Stir in the chocolate chips until melted and smooth. Pour into a large mixer bowl. Add vanilla and powdered sugar. Beat to a spread consistency. If necessary, add more powdered sugar to thicken or a few drops of milk to thin.

Coconut Snack Cake

1	box (9-ounces) Yellow cake mix
1	large egg
1½	cups flaked coconut
½	cup packed light brown sugar
1	teaspoon vanilla extract
5	tablespoons heavy cream or evaporated milk

Combine cake mix with the egg and ½ cup water as directed on package. Pour into a sprayed 8x8-inch baking dish and bake at 350° for 18 to 20 minutes or until tester inserted in center comes out clean. Place on a rack and allow to cool 10 minutes.

Combine remaining ingredients and carefully spread over cake. Place under broiler and broil about 2 minutes or until lightly browned (watch carefully, it can burn very quickly). Let cool. Makes 9 servings.

I love those little boxes of cake mixes. They are so convenient to have on hand when you don't really want a large cake or dessert.

Chocolate Fudge Cake

1	box (18.25-ounces) Chocolate Fudge cake mix
½	cup cocoa
3	large eggs
1	cup mayonnaise
1	cup semi-sweet chocolate chips
	Vanilla ice cream

In mixer bowl, combine cake mix and cocoa. Beat in the eggs and mayonnaise while gradually adding 1⅓ cups water. Beat about 2 minutes to blend. Stir in chocolate chips. Pour into a sprayed Bundt cake pan and bake at 350° for 40 to 50 minutes or until a tester inserted in center comes out clean. Cool 10 minutes, then remove and cool. Makes 12 servings.

This is a heavy dark fudge cake that is balanced by a big scoop (ok, little scoop) of vanilla ice cream.

Company Special Chocolate Cake

You will get compliments galore when you make this recipe. It looks like it came off your favorite restaurant's dessert cart. The cake isn't overly sweet, but should be paired with a raspberry or strawberry coulis, see page 203, if desired. The cake is made in a springform pan and frosted with an easy Ganache. The directions look long, but it is more in the way of explanation rather than actual work. Enjoy!

1   box (18.25-ounces) Devil's Food cake mix with pudding
½   cup cocoa
3   large eggs
1   cup mayonnaise
1   cup heavy cream
8   ounces good quality semi-sweet chocolate, coarsely chopped

In mixer bowl, combine cake mix and cocoa. Add eggs, mayonnaise and 1⅓ cups water. Beat about 1 to 2 minutes or until blended and smooth. Pour into a sprayed 10-inch springform pan. Bake at 350° for 45 to 50 minutes or until a tester inserted in center comes out clean. Cool on rack for 10 minutes. Chances are the cake will have a dome shape on top. To make the cake flat on both sides, place cake, dome side down, on a tea towel or paper towels dusted with sifted cocoa. Let cool.

Line a serving plate or cake plate with four 4-inch wide strips of wax paper. Place cake, with the bottom, nicer side up, on wax paper. The paper should extend outside of the plate; these are being used to catch the frosting drippings and should be removed after frosting has set.

Meanwhile, while cake is cooling, bring cream to a boil in a heavy saucepan. Remove from heat and add chocolate. Stir until chocolate is melted and mixture is smooth. Let cool to lukewarm, until thickened, but still liquid.

Spread over top and sides of cake; smooth with a spatula. Let set about an hour, then go back with a spatula and smooth sides. Remove wax paper. Makes 16 servings.

Walnut Shortbread

2   cups butter, softened
1   cup sugar
1   cup walnuts, finely ground
2   teaspoons vanilla extract
4   cups flour

In large mixer bowl, cream the butter and sugar until light and fluffy. Add walnuts, vanilla and flour and beat just until mixed. Spoon into a sprayed 15x10-inch jelly roll pan and spread evenly. Bake at 325° for 30 to 40 minutes or until light and golden. Cool and cut into small bars or squares. Makes about 48 cookies.

Shortbread can be addictive; you keep going back for more. This is a large recipe, but it will keep for several days if tightly covered.

Nutty Fudge Brownies

1   package (21.5-ounces) Fudge brownie mix
2¼   cups chopped pecans
2¼   cups semi-sweet chocolate chips

Mix brownie mix according to package directions.

Spread ¹/₃ of the batter, in a sprayed (bottom only) 13 x 9-inch baking pan, spreading evenly to cover. Sprinkle with ¾ cup chocolate chips and ¾ cup pecans. Repeat this step 2 more times, ending with chocolate chips and pecans. Bake at 350° for 30 to 35 minutes or until tests done. Cool and cut into bars or squares. Makes about 30 bars.

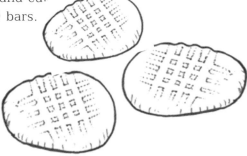

Coconut Shortbread Rolls

1	cup butter, softened
½	cup sugar
1	teaspoon vanilla extract
2	cups flour
¼	cup flaked coconut
	Powdered sugar

Variation
Omit coconut and add 1 tablespoon freshly grated lemon zest or about ⅓ cup finely chopped toasted pecans. For smaller cookies, make 2 thinner rolls.

In mixer bowl, add butter and beat slightly. Add sugar and vanilla and cream together the ingredients. Gradually add the flour and beat just until smooth. On low speed, quickly beat in the coconut. Shape mixture into a 12 to 15-inch roll. Wrap in wax paper or plastic wrap. Refrigerate until firm or overnight.

Cut into ¼-inch slices and place an inch and a half apart on an ungreased baking sheet. Bake at 350° for 12 to 15 minutes or until just lightly browned around the edges. Place on rack and cool 5 minutes. Roll in powdered sugar and let cool. Then roll again in the powdered sugar. Makes about 48 cookies.

Layered Chocolate Bars

My mother regularly supplies me with wonderful fresh pecans that are put to good use in these chocolate pecan bars.

1	package (18-ounces) sugar cookie dough, softened
2	cups semi-sweet chocolate chips
2	cups flaked coconut
1	can (4-ounces) sweetened condensed milk

Pat cookie dough evenly into a lightly sprayed 15x10-inch baking pan. Sprinkle with the chocolate chips, coconut and then the pecans. Pour condensed milk over the top. Bake at 350° for 20 to 22 minutes or until lightly browned and center is set. Makes 45 cookies.

Judy's Oatmeal Pecan Bars

4 cups quick-cooking oats
1 cup packed light brown sugar
1½ cups chopped pecans
1 cup flaked coconut
¾ cup butter, melted
¾ cup orange marmalade or apricot preserves

In a large mixing bowl, combine the oats, brown sugar, pecans and coconut. Add butter and marmalade and mix thoroughly. Press mixture evenly into a sprayed 15x10-inch jelly roll pan. Bake at 400° for 18 to 20 minutes or until light golden brown. In my oven, I have to watch the cookies every minute after 18 minutes. They can very suddenly turn too brown. Place on a rack and let cool before cutting into bars. Makes 30 bars.

Anytime I can find a good recipe to make in a 15X10-inch baking pan, I consider it a keeper. Why not make a large batch of cookies in about the same amount of time it would take to make a smaller batch.

Butter Pecan Cookies

1 cup butter, softened
¾ cup sugar
½ teaspoon baking soda
½ teaspoon white vinegar
1½ cups flour
¾ cup chopped pecans, toasted

In mixer bowl, beat butter about 1 minute. Add sugar, baking soda and vinegar and beat 7 to 8 minutes or until fluffy and turns almost white in color. By hand, stir in the flour and then the pecans. Drop onto an ungreased baking sheet making mounds slightly smaller than a walnut. Bake at 325° for 18 to 20 minutes or until lightly browned around the edges. Makes 3 dozen cookies.

These are simple ingredients that turn into a very crisp butter flavored cookie. Delicious served with a glass of milk or your favorite ice cream.

Clarine's Mexican Wedding Balls

Clarine and I both have four children and we made a lot of cookies when our children were growing up. Her version of this rich butter cookie is my favorite.

1	cup butter, softened
1¾	cups sifted powdered sugar, divided
1	teaspoon vanilla extract
¼	teaspoon salt
2¼	cups flour
1	cup rather finely chopped pecans

In mixer bowl, cream butter and the ¾ cup powdered sugar. Add vanilla and mix well. Combine salt and flour and add to creamed mixture, beating just until mixed through. Stir in pecans.

Form into 1-inch balls and place on baking sheet. Bake at 350° for 10 to 12 minutes or until lightly browned on the bottom. Place on rack and cool slightly. Roll in remaining 1 cup powdered sugar. Let cookies cool, then roll again in the powdered sugar. Makes about 4 dozen cookies.

Note: *If cookies are made ahead and frozen, you may need to roll again in powdered sugar.*

Peanut Butter Cookies

½   cup butter, softened
1   cup packed light brown sugar
1½ cups chunky peanut butter
1   large egg
1¾ cups flour
1   teaspoon baking powder

Combine butter, brown sugar and peanut butter in a mixer bowl, beating until light in color. Add the egg and mix well. Combine flour and baking powder and mix just until flour is blended. Make walnut-size balls and place on ungreased baking sheets. Flatten with a fork in a crisscross pattern. Bake at 350° for 10 to 12 minutes. Cookies should be slightly soft in the center. Makes about 36 cookies.

After School Chocolate Cookies

1   package (18.25-ounces) Milk Chocolate cake mix
½   cup oatmeal
½   cup vegetable oil
2   large eggs
½   cup raisins
1   cup semi-sweet chocolate chips

In mixer bowl, beat cake mix, oatmeal, oil and eggs just until blended. Stir in raisins and chocolate chips. The dough will be stiff. Form into balls slightly smaller than a walnut and press slightly to flatten. Place about 2 inches apart on an ungreased cookie sheet. Bake at 350° for 10 to 12 minutes. Cookies should still be soft in the center. Makes about 4 dozen cookies.

Ben's Chocolate Cookies

My grandson Ben loves to make these cookies. They are quick and easy for him to make and he takes pride in making a delicious cookie that everyone enjoys.

1   package (18.25-ounces) German Chocolate cake mix
½   cup vegetable oil
2   large eggs
½   cup flaked coconut
1   cup chopped walnuts or pecans

In a mixer bowl, beat the cake mix, oil, and eggs until blended. Add coconut and nuts and beat on low just until mixed. Drop dough by rounded teaspoons (less than walnut size), onto an ungreased baking sheet. Bake at 350° for 12 to 14 minutes. Cookies should be slightly soft in the center. Makes about 4 dozen cookies.

Cranberry Nut Shortbread Cookies

A wonderful, not too sweet, short-bread cookie.

1¼   cups butter, softened
1   cup sifted powdered sugar
2¼   cups flour
½   cup dried cranberries
½   cup chopped pecans or hazelnuts

In mixer bowl, cream the butter and sugar. Gradually add the flour and beat just until mixed. Stir in the cranberries and nuts.

Form into 1-inch balls and place on an ungreased baking sheet. Spray the bottom of a small glass, dip in sugar and flatten each ball to a little more than ¼-inch thick. Repeat for each cookie. Bake at 325° for 12 to 14 minutes or until just the bottoms are golden. Makes about 48 cookies.

Cheese Topped Strawberries

24   or so fresh strawberries
8   ounces mascarpone cheese, softened
1/3   cup sugar
1   tablespoon Grand Marnier
    Powdered sugar, optional

Try to find the small local strawberries when in season. They look better and taste better. Cut in half lengthwise.

Combine the cheese, sugar and Grand Marnier, stirring until smooth. Spoon into a pastry bag fitted with a small star tip and pipe a small amount onto the center of each strawberry. Serve as soon as possible. Makes about 48.

Extra Special:

Purchase straw-berries with nice colorful stems. Slice lengthwise, just to one side of the stems (save slices without stems for another use). Top with cheese mixture and place on serving plates. Sprinkle plate and ber-ries lightly with powdered sugar.

Apple Cinnamon Crisp

4   medium large apples, peeled and sliced (6 cups)
    Cinnamon
1¼   cups sugar, divided
¾   cup butter, divided
¾   cup flour
2   tablespoons sliced almonds

Place half the apple slices in a sprayed 8 x 8-inch baking dish. Sprinkle lightly with cinnamon and 2 tablespoons sugar. Dot with 2 tablespoons butter. Repeat layers.

Combine the remaining 1 cup sugar and the flour in a mixing bowl. Cut in the remaining ½ cup butter with two knives or a pastry blender, until about pea size. Add almonds and sprinkle mixture over apples. Bake at 350° for 40 to 50 minutes or until apples are tender. Makes 6 servings.

Lemon Raspberry Dessert

A colorful dessert for that special dinner. So easy and so few calories.

Variation: Use vanilla ice cream and raspberry purée. Top with sweetened whipped cream. Garnish with a fresh mint leaf.

2   cups raspberries (fresh or frozen)
¼   cup sugar or to taste
4   scoops lemon sorbet or sherbet
     Little julienned pieces of lemon peel for garnish.

Purée raspberries and sugar in a blender (do not let it turn to liquid). Press mixture through a sieve, collecting purée in a bowl. Discard seeds. Place sorbet in individual bowls or wine glasses. Spoon sauce over top. Garnish with lemon peel. Makes 4 servings.

Orange Marshmallow Fruit

1   package (8-ounces) cream cheese, softened
3   tablespoons fresh orange juice
1   tablespoon fresh orange zest
1   jar (7-ounces) marshmallow creme

In a mixer bowl, beat cream cheese until smooth and somewhat fluffy. Add orange juice and zest and mix until blended. Add marshmallow creme and beat on low until well mixed. Place fruit in a parfait or dessert dish. Spoon some of the cream cheese mixture over top. Garnish with additional fruit.

Fruit Combinations:

Strawberries	Kiwi	Raspberries
Blueberries	Strawberries	Honeydew
Bananas	Star Fruit	Cantaloupe

Coconut Cream Pudding

¼ cup cornstarch
1¼ cups sugar, divided
3 cups milk
4 large eggs, separated
1 teaspoon vanilla extract
1 cup flaked coconut, divided

In a heavy saucepan, combine the cornstarch with 1 cup of the sugar. Add milk and cook, over medium heat until thickened, then cook about 2 minutes. Beat the egg yolks. Add about ½ cup of the hot mixture, 1 tablespoon at a time, then add to the saucepan. Continue to cook about 3 to 4 minutes. Cool to lukewarm. Add vanilla and ¾ cup of the coconut. Pour into an ungreased 8x8-inch baking dish.

In a mixer bowl, beat egg whites to a soft peak. Add remaining ¼ cup sugar, 1 tablespoon at a time until stiff peaks form. Spread over the pudding, sealing all edges. Sprinkle remaining ¼ cup coconut over the top. Bake at 350° for 12 to 15 minutes or until the meringue is lightly browned. Cool before serving. Makes about 8 servings.

I love coconut cream pie and this is the next best thing. If you miss the crust, pour custard into a baked pie crust, spread with meringue and coconut and bake.

Ice Cream & Fruit Dessert

Ice Cream
Assorted Fruit
Caramel Sauce (see page 158)

Per Serving:

Place 3 small round scoops of ice cream in center of a luncheon size plate. Surround with piles of assorted fresh fruit and drizzle with caramel sauce.

A show stopping dessert that can be varied by your choice of ice cream and fruit.

Apple-Blackberry Crisp

Wow! The combination of apples and blackberries with a crunchy topping will have your friends clamoring for the recipe. Serve warm or room temperature and with or without a dollop of ice cream.

4	large apples, peeled and sliced (6 cups)
1½	cups blackberries, fresh or frozen
1½	cups sugar, divided
¾	cup plus 2 tablespoons flour
¾	cup butter, cubed

In a large mixing bowl, combine apples, blackberries, ½ cup sugar, and the 2 tablespoons flour, tossing to coat. Pour into a sprayed 11x7-inch baking dish.

In a small bowl, combine 1 cup sugar and the ¾ cup flour. Cut in the butter with a pastry blender or a fork until mixture resembles coarse crumbs. Sprinkle over fruit and bake at 400° for 30 to 40 minutes or until golden brown and apples are tender. Makes 6 to 8 servings.

Paulina's Lemon Sauce

I don't know why we don't make our own sauce more frequently, it is so easy. Serve over mixed fresh fruit, pound cake or Angel food cake.

3	large eggs
1	cup sugar
¼	cup butter, melted
½	cup fresh lemon juice
2	teaspoons grated lemon zest

Lightly beat eggs in the top of a double boiler. Add remaining ingredients and beat until smooth. Cook over simmering water until mixture reaches 160°, stirring frequently, about 15 minutes. At this point it should have thickened to the right consistency. Chill. Makes 2 cups.

Angel Cake & Pudding Dessert

1   box (16-ounces) Angel food cake mix
1   package (3.4-ounces) instant vanilla pudding mix
2½   cups half and half
1   tablespoon sugar
½   teaspoon rum extract
½   teaspoon vanilla extract

Mix and bake cake according to directions on package, using an Angel food tube pan. Let cool.

Meanwhile, combine remaining ingredients in a mixer bowl, beating on lowest speed for about 2 minutes. Cover and chill several hours or overnight. Stir and spoon over cake slices. Makes about 12 servings.

Variation: If desired, use fresh fruit as a garnish. You could also omit the cake and serve the sauce as a dip with fresh fruit.

Quick Cherry Cobbler

½   cup butter
1   cup sugar
1   cup flour
1½   teaspoons baking powder
¾   cup milk
1   can (20-ounces) cherry pie filling

Place butter in a 2-quart shallow baking dish and place in oven to melt (watch carefully). Combine sugar, flour, baking powder and milk, mixing just until smooth. Pour over butter. Spoon pie filling over top. Bake at 350° for 35 to 40 minutes or until lightly browned and tester inserted in center comes out clean. Makes about 6 servings.

Banana Pudding

This is comfort food that takes me back to my childhood. My mom didn't use sour cream or whipped topping and she made her pudding from scratch, but this one is so good you will be hoping for leftovers. It does make a lot though, so use a bowl that will hold at least 5 quarts or reduce the recipe.

3	packages (3.4-ounces each) instant vanilla pudding
5	cups milk
2	cups sour cream
1	container (12-ounces) frozen whipped topping, thawed
1	box (12-ounces) vanilla wafers
12	bananas, sliced

Prepare pudding mix as directed on package using the 5 cups milk. Fold in the sour cream and whipped topping.

In a 5-quart bowl, layer a third of the vanilla wafers, a third of the bananas and a third of the pudding. Repeat layers two more times. Cover and chill at least an hour before serving. Makes 12 to 15 servings, maybe more.

Tip: This is a great dish to take to a church supper, a picnic or a potluck. If desired, save a couple of the vanilla wafers to crush and sprinkle on top.

Vanilla Sherbet Dessert

A wonderful dessert you can prepare in just a few minutes. Make the dessert just before serving, but toast the coconut ahead of time.

1	pint vanilla ice cream, softened slightly
1	pint pineapple sherbet
2	teaspoons fresh orange zest
1½	tablespoons Grand Marnier liqueur
1/3	cup toasted flaked coconut

In a large mixer bowl, combine the first four ingredients; beat just until smooth and blended. Spoon into parfait or wine glasses. Sprinkle with toasted coconut. Makes 6 servings.

Tip: Leftover mixture can be frozen. The mixture will be firmer, but is equally as delicious.

Brownie Sundaes

Brownie mix
Vanilla ice cream
Caramel or Chocolate sauce, slightly heated
Chopped nuts, if desired

Prepare brownie mix as instructed on package. Let cool and cut into serving size squares. Place on a serving plate and top each dessert with a scoop of ice cream. Drizzle the dessert and some of the plate with the sauce. And for drama (we all need a little drama in our lives, don't we?) sprinkle with a little powdered sugar.

There are times when you may want a special dessert, but you just don't have a lot of time to cook. Since mixes vary, use ingredients called for on the box. To make your own sauce, see page 158.

Ice Cream & Strawberries

Vanilla ice cream
Sliced almonds
Sliced sweetened strawberries

Make desired number of ice cream balls. Quickly roll in almonds and place each in a muffin tin. Cover with plastic wrap and freeze until ready to use. Place each in a dessert dish and top with strawberries.

A delicious make ahead dessert!

Variations:

- Ice cream, coconut, hot fudge sauce

- Ice cream, sliced almonds, hot fudge sauce

- Ice cream, chopped pecans, chocolate sauce

- Ice cream, coconut, sweetened raspberries

Raisin Bread Pudding

Bread Pudding can be served with whipped cream, ice cream, rum flavored caramel sauce or just sprinkle with powdered sugar.

7	cups day old soft crust French bread, cut into 1-inch slices, then into ¾-inch cubes
¾	cup dark raisins
4	large eggs, lightly beaten
1	cup sugar
1	teaspoon vanilla extract
4	cups half and half

Place half the bread cubes in a sprayed 8x8-inch baking dish. Sprinkle raisins over top. Add remaining bread cubes.

In a large mixing bowl, combine eggs, sugar and vanilla. Gradually stir in the half and half. Pour over bread cubes. Press bread cubes down into the mixture until soaked. Cover with foil and bake 35 minutes. Remove foil and bake at 350° for 20 to 30 minutes or until center no longer jiggles and top is golden. Serve warm or room temperature. Makes 6 to 9 servings.

Note: It is sometimes hard to tell if this is really done, but it should be rather firm on top. If you prefer a drier bread pudding, add an additional 1 to 2 cups bread cubes and bake in a larger baking dish.

What is "stressed" spelled backwards?
(For answer see page 203.)

Quick Company Desserts

- Top fresh pineapple rings with a scoop of vanilla ice cream and sweetened strawberries or raspberries.

- Make an ice cream sundae by using scoops of vanilla ice cream topped with fresh pineapple cubes, sliced bananas and a drizzle of Grand Marnier or Amaretto. Top with whipped cream and garnish with toasted coconut.

- Top Pound cake or Angel food cake slices with sweetened mixed fruit, and if desired, garnish with a dollop of whipped cream.

- Make brownies in a deep dish pizza pan. Cut into pie shape wedges and serve with ice cream and chocolate sauce.

- Top purchased cheesecake slices with your favorite blueberry sauce recipe.

- Roll vanilla ice cream into serving size balls, then roll in crushed Heath candy bars. Place in muffin tins and freeze. When ready to serve, place in dessert dishes and drizzle with hot fudge sauce.

Chocolate Marbled Cheesecake

To our advantage, this dessert can be made ahead. It is a standard recipe for cheesecake with the addition of Grand Marnier and chocolate.

¼   cup graham cracker crumbs
4   packages (8-ounces each) cream cheese, softened
1⅓   cups sugar
4   large eggs
2   to 3 tablespoons Grand Marnier
3   ounces semi-sweet chocolate, melted

Sprinkle graham cracker crumbs in a lightly sprayed 9-inch springform pan. Shake to cover bottom and sides. Discard those that don't stick.

In a mixer bowl, beat cream cheese until smooth. I find that if I use the whisk attachment, I can get a creamier batter. Gradually add the sugar and beat until smooth. Add eggs, one at a time, beating just until blended. Add liqueur and beat 1½ to 2 minutes. Reserve 1¼ cups of batter. Pour remaining batter into baking pan. Watch carefully as you scrape the last bit from the bowl. If you see lumps there, scrape that part of the batter together in the bowl and beat with a hand whisk until smooth. Add to batter in pan.

Combine reserved batter with chocolate, mixing until smooth. Drizzle over top of batter. Cut through chocolate with a knife. Bake at 325° for 45 to 60 minutes or until set. You should have about a quarter size circle in the middle that moves slightly. Cool for 1 hour. Cover and refrigerate for several hours or overnight.

For the Kids.........

Popsicles

1   package (0.13-ounce) Kool Aid, any flavor
1   cup sugar
4   cups water

Combine ingredients in a pitcher, stirring until sugar dissolves. Pour into popsicle molds allowing about ¼-inch at top for mixture to expand. Insert sticks and freeze. Makes about 14 to 16 (Tupperware size) popsicles.

Fudgesicles

1   package (3.9-ounces) instant chocolate pudding mix
2   cups milk
¼   cup sugar
1   cup canned evaporated milk

In a mixer bowl, beat the pudding mix and milk for 2 minutes. Stir in the sugar and canned milk. Pour into popsicle molds, leaving about ¼-inch at top for mixture to expand. Insert sticks and freeze. Makes about 14 fudgesicles.

Every time I leave these out of a book, I get complaints. So here they are again for you to enjoy. Make plenty—you can never keep the adults away from these sweet little treats.

Hawaiian Delight Cheesecake

You will love the convenience of no-bake cheese-cakes.

2   packages (3-ounces each) soft ladyfingers
2   packages (8-ounces each) cream cheese, softened
½   cup sugar
1   can (20-ounces) crushed pineapple, well drained
1   container (8-ounces) frozen whipped topping, thawed
½   cup flaked coconut, toasted

Place ladyfingers, rounded side out, around the sides and bottom of a 9-inch springform pan. Fill in with smaller pieces where needed; you will have a few of the ladyfingers left over.

In a mixer bowl, beat the cream cheese until soft and very smooth. Gradually add the sugar and beat until fluffy. With a spatula, stir in the pineapple and fold in the whipped topping. Pour into pan and spread the top until smooth. Sprinkle with coconut. Cover with plastic wrap. Chill overnight, if you can wait, or at least several hours. Makes 8 to 10 servings.

Note: To prevent tiny lumps, make sure the cream cheese is quite soft; then beat thoroughly before adding the pineapple.

Tip: If you can't find a small 8-ounce container of whipped topping, or if you already have a larger container on hand, measure out 3½ cups for this recipe.

Ice Cream Parfaits

Chocolate ice cream
Vanilla ice cream
Crushed toffee bars

Fill desired number of glasses half full with the chocolate ice cream. Sprinkle with crushed toffee bars. Fill glasses with vanilla ice cream and sprinkle top with crushed toffee bars. If desired, serve with a nice crisp cookie.

Fill your most attractive wine or parfait glasses with ice cream and freeze for a nice frosty look.

Variations:

Vanilla ice cream, sliced sweetened strawberries

Vanilla ice cream and fresh blueberries

Orange sherbet, vanilla ice cream, mandarin oranges

Lemon sherbet, vanilla ice cream, fresh raspberries

Two or three layers of any flavor sorbet

Vanilla ice cream layered with crushed oreo cookies

Peach & Raspberry Dessert

2   cups fresh raspberries
¼   cup sugar or to taste
4   white peaches, peeled and sliced
1   pint vanilla ice cream

Sweeten raspberries with sugar to taste. Place in blender and blend just until smooth. Press mixture through a sieve to remove the seeds. Place peach slices in four dessert dishes. Top with a scoop of ice cream, then top with raspberry sauce. Makes 4 servings.

White peaches (during season) are showing up in more and more grocery stores today.

Lemon Cups

A little bit of heaven, especially after a large meal. My daughter Linda and grand-daughter Paulina said these absolutely had to go in the book.

2 large eggs, separated
1 to 2 large lemons
1 cup milk
1 tablespoon butter, melted
1 cup sugar
3 tablespoons flour

Separate the eggs, placing the whites in a mixer bowl (the whites should be at room temperature).

From the lemons, you will need ¼ cup lemon juice and 1 tablespoon lemon zest. Place in a medium mixing bowl and add remaining ingredients.

Beat the egg whites until stiff and fold into above mixture. Pour into 5 sprayed 6-ounces custard cups, filling about ¼-inch from top. Place in an 8x8-inch pan filled with about an inch of hot water. Bake at 350° for 30 to 40 minutes or until the center comes out clean. Let cool on rack; cover and chill before serving. Turn cups upside down to remove and place on dessert plates for serving. Makes 5 servings.

Peach Melba Cups

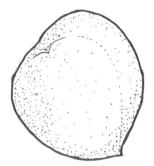

Peach halves, fresh or canned
Vanilla ice cream
Sweetened fresh raspberries or strawberries

Place each peach half in a small serving dish. Fill the center with a scoop of vanilla ice dream. Spoon berries over top and enjoy!

White Chocolate Mousse & Strawberries

4	ounces white chocolate, chopped
1½	cups heavy whipping cream
½	teaspoon, lemon, vanilla or almond extract
	Sliced strawberries, sweetened

Melt white chocolate in a small heavy saucepan over very low heat.

Meanwhile, whip cream until firm, but not stiff. Add the warm chocolate and beat until blended. Watch carefully at this point, the mixture should be a little thicker, but not curdled. Add extract. Layer with strawberries in a parfait glass or goblet.

Variations: Place a cake type ladyfinger (halved) in bottom of glass and sprinkle lightly with Amaretto or Raspberry liqueur. Then layer with raspberries, blueberries and mousse. Or place mousse in a small bowl and surround bowl with fresh strawberries and serve as a dip. It can also be served as a filling between puff pastry and sliced strawberries and placed on a bed of raspberry coulis.

What is Coulis?

Coulis is a fruit that has been sweetened, processed in a blender and then pressed through a sieve to remove the seeds. What you then have is a nice sauce to serve over or under a dessert or to decorate a plate.

D
E
S
S
E
R
T
S

Rosy Apple & Blackberry Cobbler

I like to make this in my 2½-inch 2 quart oval baking dish. Any dish will do as long as it will hold 2-quarts.

Pastry for a single pie crust

- 5 large apples, 8 cups peeled and sliced
- 2 cups blackberries; frozen is okay, do not thaw
- 1¼ cups sugar
- 1 tablespoon lemon juice

In a large mixing bowl, combine the apples, blackberries, sugar and lemon juice. Spoon into a sprayed 2-quart shallow baking dish.

Roll out pastry to fit top of baking dish with a 1-inch overhang. Place over the fruit. Turn dough under to fit to edge of inside of dish. Crimp edges, if desired. Cut 4 or 5 one-inch slits in crust to allow steam to escape. Cover dish with foil and bake at 400° for 25 minutes. Remove foil and bake for 20 to 25 minutes or until crust is golden and apples are tender. Remove and cool. Makes 8 servings.

Note: The blackberries produce a lot of juice, if a thicker sauce is preferred, add 2 tablepoons flour to apple sugar mixture. The apples will turn a beautiful deep red, which makes for a nice dish to serve on Valentine's Day. The crust is okay on the second day, but is at it's best if served on the same day made.

Apple Raisin Pie

Pastry for a double crust 9-inch pie
6   large apples (7 cups sliced)
¾   cup raisins
1   cup sugar
1   tablespoon flour
½   teaspoon cinnamon

Delicious!! This is so good my eight year old grandson Ben called me just to tell me how much he liked the pie.

Fit bottom crust in pan; trim to outside edge of plate.

Combine apples and raisins in a large bowl. Combine sugar, flour and cinnamon. Pour over apples and toss to coat. Spoon into pie shell mounding in center, and packing rather tightly.

Top with the second pie crust; trim to 1-inch from edge of plate. Fold dough under bottom crust to seal. Crimp edges, if desired. Cut about 5 one-inch slits in crust to allow steam to escape. Cover crust with foil and bake at 375° for 35 minutes. Uncover and bake for 20 to 30 minutes or until golden and apples are tender. Let cool on rack. Makes 6 to 8 servings.

Variation: This pie needs nothing else, but for special occasions I sometimes frost the top with a powdered sugar glaze: Combine 1½ cups sifted powdered sugar with 2 tablespoons water. Spread over cooled pie. Let set before cutting. Beautiful!

Note: This pie has a lot of filling in it. Use my Pie Crust recipe on page 214. You will have just enough dough for the two crusts. Purchased pie crust would not be large enough for the top crust.

Easy Sundae Pie

There are almost limitless ways to make this pie. You can vary the choice of ice cream and serve with a fruit purée rather than the chocolate sauce. You can also vary the nuts by using a different kind each time. Why not have an ice cream party and serve a variety of frozen ice cream pies with a choice of sauces, nuts and chopped candies.

1   baked 9-inch pie shell
1   quart French vanilla ice cream, softened slightly
Chocolate Sauce see Page 158
Chopped pecans

Spoon ice cream into the pie shell and spread to smooth. Cover with foil or plastic wrap and freeze.

When ready to serve, cut into wedges and pass a pitcher of chocolate sauce and a dish of nuts for serving on the pie. Or if desired, go ahead and drizzle some of the sauce over each slice of pie and around the plate. Then sprinkle the pie and the plate with a few pecans. Makes 6 to 8 servings.

Vanilla Mocha Pie

1¾   cups chocolate wafer cookie crumbs
¼   cup butter, melted
1   pint vanilla ice cream, softened
1   pint coffee ice cream, softened
1   to 2 toffee candy bars, crushed

Combine cookie crumbs and butter. Press into the bottom and sides of a 9-inch pie pan. Bake at 350° for 5 minutes and let cool on rack.

Spread vanilla ice cream over crust; place in freezer until firm. Spread coffee ice cream over top; sprinkle with crushed toffee bars. Freeze, then cover until ready to serve. It may be necessary to stand at room temperature a few minutes before cutting. Makes 6 servings.

Southern Pecan Pie

1   unbaked 9-inch pie shell
3   large eggs, lightly beaten
1   cup light corn syrup
1   cup sugar
1/3 cup butter, melted
1   cup chopped pecans

Combine eggs, corn syrup, sugar and butter. Pour into pie shell and sprinkle with pecans. Bake at 375° for 35 to 45 minutes or until the center moves just slightly when lightly shaken. Check crust several times after the first 30 minutes; if necessary cover with a sheet of foil if browning too fast. Let cool on rack. Store in the refrigerator. Makes 6 servings.

Yum! It doesn't get any sweeter than this. The recipe uses half the pecans most recipes call for, but it's all you need.

Quick Lemon Pie

1   baked 9-inch pie shell
5   large egg yolks
1   can (14-ounces) sweetened condensed milk
6   tablespoons fresh lemon juice
1   cup heavy cream, whipped with sugar to taste

Beat egg yolks lightly with a whisk. Gradually stir in the condensed milk, beating until smooth. Whisk in the lemon juice. Pour into pie shell. Cover pie with foil (this prevents crust from over browning) and bake at 350° for 10 minutes. Remove foil and bake 5 to 6 minutes. The filling should be set. Cool on rack. Makes 6 to 8 servings.

When ready to serve, top with sweetened whipped cream and garnish with fresh lemon peel or fresh berries, if desired.

If you like key lime pie, you will enjoy this recipe. I had an abundance of lemons, so I substituted lemons for the limes.

Apple Pie Delight

This is apple pie without the crust. Very rich and should be served in small portions. If desired, serve with a small scoop of vanilla ice cream.

1   cup flour
2   cups sugar, divided
½   cup chilled butter, cut into small pieces
2   tablespoons cornstarch
5   cups coarsely chopped apples

Combine the flour and 1 cup sugar, then cut in the butter until the pieces are pea size. Press half the mixture onto bottom of a sprayed 8x8-inch baking dish. Top with apples.

In a medium saucepan, combine remaining 1 cup sugar and the cornstarch. Add 1 cup water and cook, stirring frequently, until thickened. Pour over apples and sprinkle with remaining crumb mixture. Bake at 350° for about 1 hour and 20 minutes or until apples are tender and topping has browned. Serve warm. Makes 9 servings.

Pumpkin Pie

An all-time holiday favorite.

1   unbaked 10-inch deep pie crust
1   can (16-ounces) pumpkin
1   can (12-ounces) evaporated milk
¾   cup sugar
1½ teaspoons pumpkin pie spice
2   large eggs, beaten

There is a lot of filling, so make sure the pie dough is crimped high around the edge. Combine remaining ingredients and pour into pie shell and bake at 425° for 15 minutes. Reduce heat to 350° and bake 45 to 50 minutes or until a knife inserted just off center comes out clean. Let cool, then refrigerate until ready to serve. Makes 6 to 8 servings.

Apples Best for Cooking Are:

Braeburn	Gala	Jonagold
Cortland	Golden Delicious	Jonathon
Fuji	Granny Smith	Rome

Pie Tips

- For flaky pastry, use shortening, butter or lard; do not use margarine.

- Use a light hand when mixing dough and as little flour as possible for rolling.

- Use glass or dull metal pans for better browning and a flaky crust.

  If desired, brush unbaked top crust with milk, water, or melted butter, then sprinkle lightly with sugar.

- For easier slicing, allow pies to cool completely on a wire rack. Serve chilled or room temperature or reheat to lukewarm, if desired.

- Custard and cream pies should be cooled, then refrigerated.

Baked Pie Crust

Roll out the pie dough and fit (without stretching) into the pie pan. Lightly press a piece of foil to cover bottom and over the sides of the crust. Fill with dried beans or pie weights. Bake at 400° for 20 minutes. Remove from oven and carefully remove the foil and weights. Prick bottom and sides with a fork. Return to oven and bake 5 to 10 minutes or until lightly browned.

Coconut Lemon Pie

Similar to a pecan pie, but with coconut. Very rich and should be cut into small servings.

1	unbaked 9-inch pie crust
½	cup butter, melted
3	large eggs, beaten
1⅓	cups sugar
4	teaspoons lemon juice
1½	cups flaked coconut

Combine butter, eggs and sugar, mixing well. Add lemon juice and coconut. Pour into pie crust. Bake at 400° for 40 to 45 minutes or until a knife inserted just off center comes out clean. Cool on rack. Makes 8 servings.

Country Apple Tart

Note: *a purchased pie crust would not be large enough to make this recipe. Use a pie crust recipe with at least 2 cups flour. Or use recipe on page 214.*

1	unbaked pie crust (see note)
4	large apples, peeled, thinly sliced
2	tablespoons butter, diced
½	cup sugar
	Powdered sugar

Roll pastry into a 13-inch circle. Fit into a 12-inch pizza pan about ½-inch deep. Fold dough under to seal and crimp edges. Starting at outer edge arrange apple slices in a circle, overlapping slightly. When you get to the center, don't worry if it doesn't look perfect, the powdered sugar will take care of that.

Arrange butter over apples and sprinkle with sugar. Bake at 375° for 25 to 30 minutes or until apples are tender. Place under broiler and broil until apples are lightly browned, about 2 to 3 minutes. Watch carefully to prevent burning. Let cool, then sprinkle with powdered sugar. Makes 8 servings.

Blackberry Pie

Pastry for a double crust 9-inch pie

5	cups fresh or frozen blackberries
1	cup sugar
$1/3$	cup flour
1	tablespoon fresh lemon juice

Line a 9-inch pie plate with one of the crusts. Trim to outside edge of rim.

In a mixing bowl, combine remaining ingredients. Not all of the sugar mixture will stick to the berries, but that's okay. Spoon berries into the crust and sprinkle with remaining dry mixture. Top with the second pie crust; trim to 1-inch from rim of plate. Fold dough under bottom crust to seal; crimp edges. Cut 5 or 6 small slits in the crust to vent. Cover the crust with foil and bake at 400° for 40 minutes. Remove foil and bake 15 to 20 minutes or until crust is lightly browned. Allow to cool. Serve room temperature. Makes 6 servings.

Hint: Most recipes will tell you to cover the crust with foil toward the end of cooking time, if it is getting too brown. I have found if I cover the foil in the beginning, then remove it, I am less likely to over-brown the crust.

Note: Today's cooks are often intimidated by double crust pies, but after a pie or two you'll be getting raves for your desserts too.

Rustic Pies

Rustic pies are quite the rage right now and can best be described as a pie baked without a pie dish. It doesn't work with runny type pies or cream pies, but it is great made with apples, peaches and pears. The pie dough is placed on a baking sheet and the center is filled with sweetened fruit, leaving a 2-inch border from the edge of the dough. The dough is brought up and over and crimped slightly on the folds. The center of the fruit will be showing. It is then baked on the baking sheet.

This is a great way to make a pie, but most of the time I prefer doing it in a deep dish pie dish. This is easier and keeps its shape better. Just place the crust lightly in the pie dish, mound the fruit in the center leaving a border, and bring the pie dough up to partially cover the fruit; then crimp the folds lightly. Very easy and it makes beautiful pies.

Rustic Pear Pie

Dazzle your friends with this wonderful dessert. Serve each slice with a sprinkle of powdered sugar and they will be even more impressed.

1   unbaked 10-inch pie crust
4   medium fairly ripe pears, peeled, cored, sliced
½   cup sugar
3   tablespoons flour
1   tablespoon sliced almonds

Place pie crust loosely in a deep 10-inch pie dish.

In a mixing bowl, toss the pears with the sugar and flour. Spoon into the center of the pie crust, mounding the pears and leaving about a 1-inch border from the edge of the dish. Bring the crust up and over the pears, crimping the folds lightly. Not all the pears will be covered. Cover with foil and bake at 400° for 15 to 20 minutes or until pears are tender. The last 5 minutes of baking time, sprinkle with the almonds. Serve warm or room temperature. Makes 6 servings.

Rustic Apple Pie

1   unbaked 10-inch pie crust
8   cups sliced apples (Braeburns are good)
1   cup sugar, divided
1   teaspoon cinnamon
¾   cup flour
1/3   cup butter

Place pie crust loosely in a deep 10-inch pie dish, but do not shape. Fill crust with apples. Combine ½ cup sugar and cinnamon and sprinkle over apples.

Combine remaining ½ cup sugar with the flour. With a pastry blender or fork, cut in butter until crumbly, but not fine. Sprinkle over apples. Bring crust up and over the apples, crimping the folds lightly. Not all the apples will be covered. Cover pie with foil and bake at 400° for 25 minutes. Remove foil and bake about 30 minutes or until apples are tender. Watch carefully toward the end and cover with foil again, if necessary, to prevent burning. Let cool on rack. Makes 6 to 8 servings.

Rustic pies are all the rage right now and are usually baked free form on a baking sheet, but I like to place the dough in a pottery dish, then shape and bake.

Pottery Dish

My favorite pottery dish cost less than six dollars and can be found in the garden department of large home center stores. It is 10-inches in diameter and about 2 to 2½-inches deep. These are saucers for larger planting pots. Purchase the ones that are glazed and do a lead test. I use them not only for pies, but also for yeast rolls, casseroles and potato dishes.

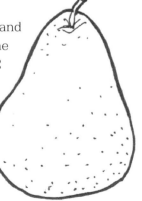

Pie Crust Chart

Crust	Crumbs	Sugar	Butter
Graham Crackers	1½ cups	¼ cup	½ cup
Pretzels	1⅓ cups	2 Tablespoons	⅓ cup
Vanilla Wafers	1¼ cups	———	⅓ cup
Chocolate Wafers	1¼ cups	———	⅓ cup

Pie Crust

Makes two single crust pies or one double crust pie. Some recipes will tell you this amount of dough would make 3 single crusts, but that is pushing it somewhat. Since I don't always roll a perfect circle, I like a little extra dough to work with.

3   cups flour
1½ teaspoons salt
1   cup plus 2 tablespoons shortening
6   tablespoons cold water (approximate)

In a mixing bowl, combine the flour and salt. Add shortening and cut in with a pastry blender or a fork until mixture is the consistency of small peas.

Sprinkle center of flour with 1 tablespoon water. Stir with a fork until water is absorbed. Add 1 tablespoon water at a time to another dry part of the mixture, mixing to blend. Continue until all the mixture is moist enough to hold together. You may need to use more or less water than called for.

Shape dough into a smooth ball and divide in half. Shape each half into a ball and flatten to about an inch thick. The dough is ready to roll or can be wrapped and refrigerated about 30 minutes. Dough can be made a day or two ahead, but may be slightly harder to roll out: (Let stand 10 minutes before rolling.)

Index

Index

Index

SANDWICHES

SEAFOOD

SOUPS, CHOWDERS & STEWS

Index

Great Meals Begin With Six Ingredients Or Less

Six Ingredients or Less Families on the Go - Our quickest and easiest recipes yet. Designed to get you in and out of the kitchen fast. 288 pages, $16.95

Six Ingredients or Less Diabetic - Over 400 delicious diabetic conscious, low-fat and low-carb recipes. Includes nutritional anaylsis and diabetic exchanges. 288 pages, Comb bound, $18.95.

Six Ingredients or Less Low-Carb - Over 600 delicious easy recipes to help you creatively cook with 0 to 6 net carbs per recipe. Includes nutritional analysis. 288 pages, Comb bound, $18.95.

Six Ingredients or Less Cookbook - Revised and expanded edition. Over 600 recipes and 352 pages. Quick and easy recipes from everyday cooking to delicious company entertaining. Sections include: Appetizers, Breads, Cookies, Desserts, Beef, Poultry, Vegetables and many more. $16.95.

Six Ingredients or Less Light & Healthy - Devoted to great cooking your family will love, and they'll never know the recipes are good for them. Recipes include nutritional analysis for calories, fat grams, cholesterol, sodium, etc. 224 pages, $12.95.

Six Ingredients or Less Pasta and Casserole - A 224 page cookbook for today's busy lifestyles. The original and lowfat version is given for each recipe. $14.95.

Six Ingredients or Less Slow Cooker - 224 Pages of Quick and Easy stress free meals by letting the Slow Cooker do the work for you. $14.95.

Remember, Cookbooks Make Great Gifts!

SIXINGREDIENTSORLESS.COM

If you cannot find our cookbooks at your local store, you can order direct. Copy or fill out the order blank below and return, with your check, money order, VISA or MC number to:

SIX INGREDIENTS OR LESS
PO BOX 339, Moyie Springs, ID 83845
1-800-423-7184

Families on the Go	(____) # of copies	**$16.95 each**	$_____
Diabetic Cookbook	(____) # of copies	**$18.95 each**	$_____
Low-Carb Cookbook	(____) # of copies	**$18.95 each**	$_____
Six Ingredients or Less	(____) # of copies	**$16.95 each**	$_____
Six Ingredients or Less Light & Healthy	(____) # of copies	**$12.95 each**	$_____
Six Ingredients or Less Pasta & Casseroles	(____) # of copies	**$14.95 each**	$_____
Six Ingredients or Less Slow Cooker	(____) # of copies	**$14.95 each**	$_____
Plus Postage & Handling (First book $3.50, each add't book, add $1.50)			$_____
Washington residents add 8.5% sales tax or current tax rate			$_____
Total			$_____

Please Print or Type
(Please double-check addition, differences will be billed)

Name_____ Phone (____)_____

Address_____

City_____ State _____ Zip_____

MC or Visa _____ Exp_____

Signature_____

www.sixingredientsorless.com
email: info@sixingredientsorless.com